Literary Theory:
A Practical Introduction

To *E. P. Kuhl* and *Robert Scholes*
for teaching me how to read

LITERARY THEORY:

A Practical Introduction

Readings of
William Shakespeare, *King Lear*
Henry James, "The Aspern Papers"
Elizabeth Bishop, *The Complete Poems 1927–1979*
Toni Morrison, *The Bluest Eye*

Michael Ryan

BLACKWELL
Publishers

First published 1999
Reprinted 1999 (twice), 2001

Blackwell Publishers Inc.
350 Main Street
Malden, Massachusetts 02148
USA

Blackwell Publishers Ltd
108 Cowley Road
Oxford OX4 1JF
UK

Library of Congress Cataloging-in-Publication Data

Ryan, Michael, 1951–
    Literary theory: a practical introduction: readings of William Shakespeare, *King Lear,* Henry James, "The Aspern papers," Elizabeth Bishop, *The complete poems 1927–1979,* Toni Morrison, *The bluest eye* / by Michael Ryan.
        p.   cm.
    Includes bibliographical references and index.
    ISBN 0–631–17275–0 (alk. paper). — ISBN 0–631–17276–9 (pbk.: alk. paper)
      1. Literature—Philosophy.   2. Literature—History and criticism—Theory, etc.   I. Title.
    PN45.R93   1999
    801—dc21   98–28722
                                                   CIP

British Library Cataloguing in Publication Data

A CIP catalogue record for this book is available from the British Library.

Commissioning editor: Andrew McNeillie
Development Editor: Alison Dunnett
Desk Editor: Brigitte Lee
Production Manager/Text Designer: Lisa Eaton
Picture Researcher: Leanda Shrimpton

Typeset in 10½ on 12½pt. Ehrhardt
by Ace Films Ltd, Frome, Somerset
Printed in Great Britain by T.J. International, Padstow, Cornwall

This book is printed on acid-free paper

Contents

Preface   viii

Acknowledgments   x

1 Formalism   **1**
  1.1   Introduction   1
  1.2   A Russian Formalist Reading of *King Lear*   6
  1.3   Suggestions for a New Critical Reading of *King Lear*   11
  1.4   A Formalist Reading of Elizabeth Bishop's "The Moose"   12
  1.5   Suggestions for a Formalist Reading of Elizabeth Bishop's "At the Fishhouses"   24

2 Structuralism   **26**
  2.1   Introduction   26
  2.2   A Structuralist Reading of *King Lear*   29
  2.3   Suggestions for a Structuralist Reading of "The Aspern Papers"   33
  2.4   Suggestions for a Structuralist Reading of Elizabeth Bishop's "The Map"   34

3 Psychoanalysis   **35**
  3.1   Introduction   35
  3.2   A Psychoanalytic Reading of Elizabeth Bishop's "In the Village" and "Sestina"   38
  3.3   A Psychoanalytic Reading of *The Bluest Eye*   44
  3.4   Suggestions for a Psychoanalytic Reading of *King Lear*   49
  3.5   Suggestions for a Psychoanalytic Reading of "The Aspern Papers"   50

Contents

4 Marxism   **52**
4.1 Introduction   52
4.2 A Marxist Reading of *King Lear*   54
4.3 Suggestions for a Marxist Reading of "The Aspern Papers"   62
4.4 Suggestions for a Marxist Reading of Elizabeth Bishop's "A Miracle for Breakfast"   64
4.5 Suggestions for a Marxist Reading of *The Bluest Eye*   65

5 Post-Structuralism, Deconstruction, Post-Modernism   **67**
5.1 Introduction   67
5.2 A Post-Structuralist Reading of *King Lear*   76
5.3 A Post-Structuralist Reading of Elizabeth Bishop's "Crusoe in England"   89
5.4 Suggestions for a Post-Structuralist Reading of Elizabeth Bishop's "Over 2,000 Illustrations and a Complete Concordance"   98
5.5 Suggestions for a Post-Structuralist Reading of *The Bluest Eye*   98

6 Feminism   **101**
6.1 Introduction   101
6.2 A Feminist Reading of "The Aspern Papers"   104
6.3 Suggestions for a Feminist Reading of *King Lear*   113
6.4 Suggestions for a Feminist Reading of Elizabeth Bishop's "Roosters"   113
6.5 Suggestions for a Feminist Reading of *The Bluest Eye*   114

7 Gender Studies, Queer Theory, Gay/Lesbian Studies   **115**
7.1 Introduction   115
7.2 A Gender Reading of *King Lear*   118
7.3 Suggestions for a Gender Reading of Elizabeth Bishop's "In the Waiting Room"   126
7.4 Suggestions for a Gender Reading of *The Bluest Eye*   127

8 Historicism   **128**
8.1 Introduction   128
8.2 An Historicist Reading of *King Lear*   131
8.3 Suggestions for an Historicist Reading of "The Aspern Papers"   139
8.4 Suggestions for an Historicist Reading of Elizabeth Bishop's "Twelve O'Clock News"   142
8.5 Suggestions for an Historicist Reading of *The Bluest Eye*   144

9 Ethnic, Post-Colonial, and International Studies **147**

9.1 Introduction 147

9.2 A Post-Colonial Reading of Elizabeth Bishop's "Brazil, January 1, 1502" 149

9.3 Suggestions for an Ethnic Studies Reading of Elizabeth Bishop's "Faustina, or Rock Roses" 154

9.4 Suggestions for an Ethnic Studies Reading of *The Bluest Eye* 155

Index 156

Preface

Literary theory is both renowned and feared for its difficulty. A recent *New York Times* article described French theorist Jacques Derrida as incomprehensible, and in reaction to theory, an entire new sub-profession of disgruntled literature professors has developed in the US. When great tidal changes occur of the kind that have transformed literary study over the past few decades and shifted the edifice of criticism off its old foundations, it is understandable that those with an investment in the old vocabularies and the displaced paradigms should take issue, although the aggressive hostility of journalists and academics alike makes one wonder if something more than a choice of schools of literary criticism is at stake. Whatever the truth may be, literary theory is a field that begs for clarification, and it is for that reason that I wrote this book. I had taught theory as theory for years when, around 1980, I decided for the first time to incorporate primary works of literature into my theory courses. I felt that students would be aided by seeing theory at work in the practical reading of texts. And I felt that the important differences between theories – the way each illuminated a different aspect of a work of literature – would be clearer if they were comparatively applied to the same literary work. But it turned out to be difficult to find readings from varying critical perspectives of the same work. Each school seemed to favor certain kinds of texts, with, for example, the deconstructionists favoring symbolic poetry and the Marxists realist novels. I decided at that point – around the mid-1980s – to write my own readings of the same text, each of which would assume a different critical stance or theoretical perspective. Blackwell Publishers liked the idea of a collection of practical applications that might serve as a companion text to Terry Eagleton's *Literary Theory: An Introduction*, and we signed a contract in 1988. The book might have been finished and published back then had not children come along to interrupt the process. In addition, I realized that the larger project of introducing literary theory to new generations of students would also require an up-to-date anthology with selections from the schools of theory that were expanding the range of critical inquiry even as I wrote my practical introduction. With Julie Rivkin, I therefore set about constructing *Literary Theory: An Anthology* (Blackwell), which appeared in 1997 and which ideally should be used in conjunction with this book. In teaching theory, I usually ask students to read a selection from the anthology as well as an application from this book of that particular theory. In class, we then discuss how the theory might work in reading one or more of the other primary literary texts used in the course. Those works are Shakespeare, *King Lear*, Henry James, "The Aspern Papers," Elizabeth Bishop, *The Complete Poems* and *The Collected Prose*, and Toni Morrison, *The Bluest Eye*. I space out the reading of the primary texts over the first few weeks of the term, and we re-visit each work from a number of different perspectives throughout the course. While initially I felt some hesitation about (and heard quite a bit of criticism for) aspiring to be all things theoretical to all people, I have learned that if students are to be expected to learn to practice different approaches, then teachers themselves must impose the same expectation on themselves. And what one realizes in the process is that not only must one be many things to teach the range of critical approaches, but one can be many things.

Part of the difficulty not so much *of* theory as *with* theory is that it forces us out of our habitual perspectives and invites us to adopt the very different perspectives of those who have been the unacknowledged victims of the dominant ways of seeing, both in the world at large and in literary study in particular. To write and to read a book like this is therefore to pretend, momentarily, at least, to be something other than what one is. And one outcome of this process, I would hope, is that "what one is" might come to seem a less settled matter than one thinks.

Acknowledgments

I am grateful to Jay Clayton, Margaret Homans, and Julie Rivkin for their extremely helpful suggestions and advice.

CHAPTER 1

Formalism

1.1 Introduction

One of the first major schools of literary study in the twentieth century – Formalism – took the relatively simple, though at the time quite revolutionary, position that what a work of literature is about – its content – is related to how it is put together – its form. We could not fully know the meaning of *King Lear* if we did not attend to the way it is constructed as a double plot in which an old king dies in one plot while a new one is born in the other. The form of the dual plot is required for the meaning of the play to be fully enunciated. According to this formalist approach – usually associated with the American New Critics – form is an essential component of content.

Other early twentieth-century formalists took the argument further: literature is nothing but form, and content is merely an effect of form. The dual plot of *King Lear* does not express a meaning that is then communicated by its formal apparatus; rather, the meaning is generated by the way form shapes dramatic action. The play is nothing but this formal arrangement.

Regardless of whether we think form expresses content or content is an effect of form, all of us have probably been trained to read literature as formalists simply by virtue of having learnt how to read literature at all in the first place. That is, we learn to read by attending to the way meaning inheres in the formal features of a text. For many of us in US secondary schools and colleges, becoming students of literature meant noticing how Hamlet's soliloquies, which indicate a thematic failure to act while deferring, in a formal sense, the ongoing action of the play, bear a relation to the tragic content, how the multiple narrators of *Wuthering Heights* create a sense of unknowability appropriate to the novel's romantic evocation of life beyond the grave, how the self-consciously fragmented lines of *The Waste Land* embody Eliot's pessimism regarding modernity, or how Conrad's use of an internal narrator in *Heart of Darkness* creates irony in the story of imperialism.

Formalism might also be called a necessary first step in any study of literature. Before one can study *The Scarlet Letter* from a historicist perspective by asking how its argument for moral compromise relates to the debates in America in the 1850s regarding the Great Compromise over slavery, or from a feminist perspective by asking how its depiction of Hester Prynne might be considered a criticism of such contemporary women writers as Margaret Fuller, or from a Post-Structuralist perspective by asking how it critiques moral absolutism through an inquiry into the plurality of meanings given the scarlet "A," one must first read the work and become aware of the unfolding of meaning through the deployment of such literary techniques and procedures as narrative perspective, the metaphoric use of location, character construction, and symbolism. Simply to open the book and to begin reading is to be placed before a closed prison door with a wild rose growing next to it and a group of community gossips standing about. It is to be involved in a narrative perspective, to be presented with clearly symbolic objects, to meet characters who represent a position or argument regarding the events of the story, and to be provided a language of understanding that constructs the reader's awareness in a particular way. To know what the novel means is to be involved in its form, in the way it is put together.

The method of formal analysis has not always occupied so central a place in literary study. Before the twentieth century, the study of literature was concerned more with biography and history than with the study of narrative technique or the use of sound in verse. *King Lear* would be studied not for its double plot, but for how it covertly referred to intrigues between Parliament and King James. All of that changed as the result of the work of two separate groups of formalist scholars – the Russian Formalists, whose major works date from the teens and twenties, and the American New Critics, whose work spans the period from the thirties to the sixties.

A group of Russian linguists and critics – Viktor Shklovsky, Boris Tomashevsky, Roman Jakobson – were the first to argue that the formal dimension of literature – everything from rhythm patterns in poetry to narrative strategies in fiction – should be the primary concern of literary study. Such procedures and techniques make literature different from other kinds of writing such as philosophy or sociology whose purpose is to communicate ideas or to name facts. Literary language differs from these other kinds of speech, which are characterized by the referential or denotative use of language and by the transparency of form in relation to content, in that it uses language connotatively to give rise to secondary meanings and in that it foregrounds form. To read a poem is to read an arrangement of sounds and words that looks different and that means differently from ordinary speech or the ordinary use of the same words. Literature changes ordinary language by roughening it up so that the words draw attention to themselves. Because the usual denotative use of language to name facts or communicate ideas directly is thereby disrupted, literature defamiliarizes the world. Literary language ruptures rote patterns of perception and makes strange a reality that normal language has rendered invisible to us. Tolstoy, for example, describes a flogging with a geometrical detachment and a calculated precision that forces the reader to see anew – and to feel the shock of – a practice that might otherwise seem routine and acceptable.

The Russian Formalists argued provocatively that form subsumes content and that the history of transformations in literature is due entirely to formal metamorphoses. They argued that form subsumes content because they felt no ideas exist in literature outside or apart from the mechanics of the text. Tolstoy may have had an idea regarding flogging that he wished to communicate, but the idea comes to the reader as an effect of language and narrative. Before the reader can experience the idea "flogging is unjust," he or she must experience the inappropriately banal language Tolstoy uses to describe such punishment. The idea does not exist apart from the defamiliarizing effect of that particular language use.

The Russian Formalists also argued that the evolution of new literary forms changes what literature is about. By distinguishing between the narrative or the way a story is told and the story or series of events the narrative recounts, they made possible an understanding of how new modes of story-telling make possible new contents. If the way a story is told determines what it is about, then a change in the mode or procedure of story-telling can open up new possibilities of content. The form of the medieval quest romance – long poems with chivalric characters and religious themes – determines the range of characters and ideas one would be likely to encounter in such works. Cervantes' use of a picaresque narrative style in *Don Quixote*, a new post-romance kind of novel which strings adventures together with seeming randomness, is a formal development that accounts for or motivates the pliability of his hero, Don Quixote. The new form makes possible a new content.

The Russian Formalist critics were also concerned with defining and describing the specific qualities and characteristics of particular genres and discourses. The early Formalists concentrated on the use of rhythm and sound repetition in poetry. A later writer in the Formalist tradition, Mikhail

Bakhtin, focused on the specific characteristics of novelistic discourse. He argued that while poetry is monological – that is, narrated in a single voice from a single perspective – novels are heteroglossic or multi-voiced. They incorporate different modes of speech through the narrator's adoption of a character's point of view, through embedded commentary on the fictional events, through the use of irony and parody, and through hidden polemics against other writers. He also studied what he called carnivalesque discourse, especially the incorporation of the language of the medieval carnival in the work of Rabelais, and argued that carnivalesque language, with its ribald bodily humor, represented a significant overturning of the high seriousness of official medieval culture, which thrived on fear.

The Russian Formalist method of reading is concerned with describing the procedures and techniques of a literary work. Those might include narration and plot construction in fiction or the use of rhyme, rhythm, euphony, and alliteration in poetry. A Russian Formalist reading would also be alert to how texts disrupt our expectations by using language in new ways. *The Adventures of Huckleberry Finn*, for example, places us in the unhabitual linguistic and experiential universe of an uneducated ragamuffin who lives on the edge of respectability and does not have much respect for "sivilization." Rather than think of form as the embodiment of meaning, such a reading would consider meaning to be an effect or function of the formal procedures of the work.

The American New Critics pursued a different formalist agenda from the 1930s through the 1960s. They shared with the Russian Formalists a sense that literary language (especially poetry) is of a different nature than ordinary practical speech, but they were more interested in the way such language expresses universal truths than in performing a scientific description of literary forms. Moreover, rather than study entire genres, they performed close readings of individual works. By close reading, they meant that critics should attend to the texture of imagery and language in a given work rather than seek out its extra-textual biographical or historical referents. The work itself is the proper object of criticism, and the New Critics felt that great works are characterized by an organic unity of form and meaning. Because language and meaning are welded together, to elucidate the texture of imagery in a work is necessarily to describe its meaning. The two exist inextricably together.

The New Critics saw literary language, poetic language especially, as providing an almost mystical experience of coherence in which opposites – language and meaning, spirit and matter, content and form, the particular and the universal – are reconciled. Literary language possesses connotative potentials that distinguish it from ordinary language, which is restricted to denotation or the naming of single things with single words. Literary language uses complex tropes and images such as metaphor, symbol, irony, and paradox to generate secondary meanings that cannot be rendered in simple, straightforward denotative speech. This capacity allows literature to carry out a reconciliation of the normally opposed realms of the universal and the particular. Particular words or images can then be used to express universal meanings. This reconciliation of contraries is what distinguishes literature from other kinds of language use. The purpose of criticism is to describe how universal meaning and specific uses of literary language are welded together to form perfect organic unities.

Paradox is the trope that most characterizes poetry, since all poetry fuses the ideal or spiritual with the worldliness of language. Cleanth Brooks, for example, carefully studies the language of such poems as Keats' "Ode on a Grecian Urn" to find paradoxical images like "sylvan historian" and "Cold pastoral" that spoke of such opposites as fluidity and stillness, the ideal and the ordinary, eternal perfection and temporal decay, and life and death at once. In such paradoxical images Brooks finds stated the entire meaning of the poem: that the frozen world of art (the urn) is paradoxically more dynamic than life precisely because it is frozen. In art, one grasps essential truths that are outside history and are timeless, and such truths are always beautiful; though they seem lifeless and dead, they paradoxically possess eternal life because they never decay or change. In their deathly stillness, the dynamism of what is living is preserved forever. The poem thus reconciles opposites, and as an aesthetic experience of coherence, it provides a lived example of the theme it enunciates.

A New Critical method of reading would attend to the verbal patterns of a given work, what the New Critics called its texture, and it would relate those patterns to the meanings the work both enunciates and instantiates. While this method might seem to favor the tropes and imagery of poetry, it also applies to narrative design and dramatic technique. *The Scarlet Letter* begins from the perspective of gossips commenting on an imprisoned adulteress for reasons that bear on the meaning of the novel. The narrative form embodies a major conflict of the novel – the difference between redemption that is achieved through personal means and one that is imposed by a community. Hawthorne begins with the gossips to portray a negative version of communal imposition, and that formal choice has the effect or function of making the personal alternative, figured appropriately as behind a closed door in the opening scene, seem more appealing. The universal idea that personal redemption is better than an accommodation to external communal norms is instantiated in the concrete and particular emblem of the symbolically arranged figures in the opening scene.

Both schools of formalist criticism succeeded in making the study of technique, procedure, construction, and language – form, in short – central to literary study. As we shall see later in this book, even literary scholars whose approaches emphasize history or politics have come to integrate the formal study of literature – albeit a modified or inflected version – to their work.

Formalism itself, however, has been criticized for failing to take into account its own implicit politics and for not justifying the separation of formal from other, more social or political concerns. To isolate form – either as an essential feature of content or as the be-all and end-all of literature – is to make a political and ideological decision that places such things as a literary work's connection to a world defined by violently maintained hierarchies of gender, class, and race in a secondary position in relation to form. Indeed, Russian Formalism might be read from a feminist perspective as exemplifying a form of abstract thinking characteristic of a male-dominated intellectual world from which issues of gender politics were successfully purged. And the New Criticism might be understood from a Marxist perspective as giving expression to a conservative ideology that emerged in response to twentieth-century social changes and to Modernism, a movement that favored experimentation over the traditional aesthetic and religious practices and beliefs favored by the New Critics. Formalism, for all its seeming innocence as a simple attentiveness to "literature on the page," is not innocent. Indeed, everything that follows in this book – from historical and political approaches to gender and ethnic approaches – might just as easily come first and be understood as the necessary precursors to any formal study of literature.

1.2   A Russian Formalist Reading of *King Lear*

A Russian Formalist reading of *King Lear* might begin by noting that the play defamiliarizes some of the most important assumptions of its world. That world rested on the idea that there was a natural hierarchy of rank in society, with commoners at the bottom and the nobility and the king at the top. It was a world held together by rules of deference and respect, as well as by certain stylized language procedures, codified modes of address, and distinguishing titles. Only certain kinds of action were conceivable within this world of stable conventions, procedures, and stereotyped behaviors, and only certain kinds of speech were acceptable or legitimate. *Lear* disrupts these assumptions both dramatically and verbally. Characters who should, according to the rules, tell the truth and speak respectfully, lie to and insult their social superiors. A king, who should be a moral guide and model, breaks the rules of his social world by refusing a dowry and banishing a daughter.

The audience is then taken to the unexpected and unfamiliar terrain of madness and exile, where normal speech further erodes and degrades into babble and ribald innuendo.

What is the effect of defamiliarization in the play? A core theme of *Lear* is the battle between feeling and obligation, with Lear representing the obligation to respond in certain ways while Cordelia represents the priority of feeling over external obligation. The play defamiliarizes Lear's position and all the linguistic markers that accompany it, and the narrative moves him into a position of madness and social privation where the rules of social obligation come to appear arbitrary and conventional. It is only when the artificiality of the conventions is revealed to him that Lear can move over to the other side of the initial thematic tension and realize that feeling must precede obligation.

A Russian Formalist would also attend to the specifically literary procedures that allow the story to be told and the themes to be enunciated. For example, rather than begin with Lear, as one might expect from the title of the play, the play opens instead by telling his story indirectly through the voices of Kent and Gloucester. What are some of the implications of this procedure? We learn from the conversation between Kent and Gloucester that Lear is hard to know, and, as we learn later, he also hardly knows himself, a fault that will have tragic effects. The motif of indirect presentation is thus the first formal motivator of the theme of faulty knowledge. No one can be known directly or in themselves (an impossibility since it would mean becoming that person), and what we can know of others must come to us in indirect or mediated form, usually through what is said to us in language. But language, as we soon learn in the scenes that follow, is a medium without any built-in guarantees of verisimilitude; it can therefore give rise to errors in knowledge, and it can be used deliberately to provoke such errors. As a representation rather than a thing – words rather than actual ideas or feelings – language can be either a true expression or representation of feelings and ideas, or it can be a false semblance of something true. It can be either Kent's simple, plain, and direct statement of dutiful affection, or it can be Goneril and Regan's exaggerated protestations of affection that harbor no substantive equivalents to the words used. The procedure of indirect presentation thus generates themes or issues or ideas that will prove central to the concerns of the play. By placing the audience in a position of faulty knowledge (we only partially know Lear at the outset and see him only obliquely), the play formally executes one of its principal thematic concerns, and it alerts the audience that the inscrutability of others' personalities and hidden desires may be one of the major motivators of plot action.

The procedure of indirect presentation also, of course, decenters and distances Lear as a character. We are instructed by the procedure not to take his speeches in the following scene as seriously as we might had he been presented to us directly, in his own voice, as it were. His words are deprived of some of the authority they might have possessed had not the qualifier of indirect presentation shaped his entry, and we are positioned to consider him a character to be observed and perhaps even criticized rather than identified with.

A Russian Formalist would also notice the bawdy language of the opening dialogue, which is rife with puns and ribald innuendo. Does this use of language have a function or motivation? The low language of gossip in the initial dialogue between Kent and Gloucester is strikingly at odds with the language of high statecraft in the rest of the scene, but the high speech is associated with Lear's delusions of absolute authority and with his daughters' false flattery. And as we learn in later scenes, low, popular speech, in the form either of the Fool's instructive taunts or of Edgar's mad speeches, has a crucial redemptive effect on Lear. A victim of flattery, with its inflated and false images, he learns from the Fool and from Edgar, both of whose speech is laced with raw, literal, bodily imagery, the truth of what things are really like, without the adornment of rhetorical inflation or artifice.

The low or bawdy speech of the opening dialogue, therefore, which at first has a defamiliarizing effect that upsets our expectations regarding a tragedy about kings, in fact instantiates a crucial procedure at work throughout the play – the use of low language to deflate the pretensions of high language and to guide perceptions toward truth and away from falseness. In this initial instance, it prepares us to hear Lear's inflated high speech in the rest of the first scene as being at odds with the more plain style associated with Gloucester's honest acknowledgment of adulterous reality in the opening dialogue, a style that will be linked throughout the play with virtue and innate nobility.

The motif of the sexual pun in the dialogue between Kent and Gloucester ("Do you smell a fault?", "I cannot conceive you") has a similar function. The puns suggest that words can have two meanings, one hidden or implicit, the other explicit. Such linguistic duality is at the origin of the political crisis in the play. Goneril and Regan can deceive Lear only because words can have more than one meaning (with the initial word in question being, significantly enough, "conceive"), and the public or explicit meaning may have nothing to do with the private and withheld meaning.

Such duality also bears importantly on the play's theme of true nobility or virtue. The topic of the initial conversation between Kent and Gloucester is the difference between Gloucester's two sons – the illegitimate Edmund and the legitimate Edgar. As the same word can have two meanings, so the same object – a son – can also have two quite different social meanings. Gloucester's refusal to accept the inverse valuation of his sons – one legitimate, the other illegitimate – which feudal society imposes (Edgar, he says, is "no dearer in my account") foreshadows a failure to differentiate truly noble from falsely noble, properly born from improperly bred, which will be central to the play. In the rest of the scene, Lear fails to properly distinguish Goneril and Regan on the one hand, and Cordelia on the other. And he does so because he fails to read their speeches as Kent and Gloucester read each other's speeches in the opening dialogue, which is to say, as puns, as acts of language with dual meanings. Lear fails to read Goneril and Regan's praise as expressions of dislike and Cordelia's silence as an expression of love.

Of the opening dialogue, finally, a Russian Formalist critic might note that the action occurs out of the way of the principal events with which the play is initially concerned. Compared to the declarations of Lear that follow immediately, it has more the quality of an aside. Moreover, its topics are an event (adultery, illegitimate birth) which occurred behind the scenes of legitimate social action and a hidden intention kept from public view ("it appears not which of the Dukes he values most"). The behind-the-scenes quality of the opening dialogue might thus be said to dramatize the problem of hidden intentions (kept behind the scenes of flattering statements) that will bring about Lear's downfall. As it is difficult to decipher Lear's thoughts, so also will it be difficult to know Goneril and Regan's real feelings. And as it is difficult to know the difference between the legitimate and the illegitimate son and heir, so also it will be difficult to know where true nobility lies – in the frank Cordelia or in the flattering Goneril and Regan.

That the play begins off center stage suggests the position it will advocate in these debates: truth is not a matter of external show and consists not of staged words but of true feeling that necessarily occurs out of view – "Speak what we feel, not what we ought to say." Legitimate nobility or virtue will also prove to be a matter of internal noble qualities rather than external public display. The fore-stage, the play itself suggests in its opening background dialogue, is a realm of deception. The motif of indirect presentation through an initial aside therefore serves an important function. It frames what follows as a dramatization of the play's lesson regarding truth and value, and its own use of language and staging suggests already what the point of that lesson will be.

That one dialogue could generate a number of ideas regarding its function in the play suggests that an exhaustive reading of all the literary procedures and techniques of the play would require considerable time. It also suggests just how important each procedure is in the creation of a functioning literary work.

We will conclude our application of Russian Formalism by noting how the work of Mikhail Bakhtin bears on the play. *King Lear* is a heteroglossic text that incorporates a variety of modes of speech. The opening dialogue, for example, is characterized by a mix of court gossip and ribald innuendo, the rest of the scene by a conflict between courtly flattery on the one hand and noble plainness on the other. Lear's speech at least initially constitutes an idiom of its own – overly ornate, classical in its references, and bombastic. Edmund uses words like "business" and "prosper" that associate him with the language of the upwardly mobile middle class of merchants. Edgar's styles of speech vary from situation to situation. He adopts the speech of beggarly madness with Lear, speaks as a Somerset peasant with Oswald, and finally assumes the sententious style of true nobility after he defeats Edmund.

In Bakhtin's terms, Lear's speech qualifies as an authoritative discourse, what Bakhtin calls the language of the fathers. It demands acknowledgment – "Go tell the Duke and 's wife I'd speak with them, / Now, presently. Bid them come forth and hear me." Its classical references suggest an organic relationship to the past and to a tradition from which it derives its authority – "Now, by Apollo . . ." Its meanings are singular and monological, unmixed with any other discourse. Lear refuses to modify his speech when cautioned by others, and his authoritarian intention to make word and thing match perfectly is most evident in his curses, which seek to perform what they say: "Into her womb convey sterility; / Dry up in her the organs of increase."

Lear's breakdown into madness occurs predictably as a breakdown of language. His speech loses its inflexibility, ceases to command, and mixes with the speech of others, especially Edgar. All of these losses, however, are gains in the overall process of recovery. Edgar's more flexible speech (which resembles Bakhtin's internally persuasive speech) is important in this regard. Edgar is capable of playing with the contexts and borders of speech, transforming his speech to suit the person he addresses and adapting a variety of alien idioms as his own. With his father, he first appears as Tom O'Bedlam, then as a passerby. His flexible transitions offer a contrast to Lear, who is incapable of adapting himself or his speech to different situations and suffers in consequence.

Like a capacity for heteroglossia, the power of dialogization (the citation or stylization and rendering conventional of another discourse) is associated with the affirmative characters in the play. In the first scene, Cordelia dialogizes her sisters' exercises in flattery by commenting on them in asides: "What shall Cordelia speak? Love and be silent. / . . .I am sure my love's more ponderous than my tongue." In so doing, she affirms the values of the play – that truth is a matter of feeling rather than words – and she undermines her sisters' efforts at least in the eyes of the reader or viewer by underscoring their conventionality. Kent, a parallel character to Cordelia in that he also favors plain speech over ornate flattery, does something similar when in 2.2 he mockingly imitates the court style of flattery: "Sir, in good faith, in sincere verity, / Under th'allowance of your great aspect . . ."

Such acts of dialogization resemble the acts of verbal carnivalesque degradation that Bakhtin locates in the work of Rabelais, and fittingly, another parallel character to Kent is the Fool, who is a carnivalesque figure. Indeed, *Lear* is carnivalesque to the extent that, as a narrative of death and rebirth, it poses against an old order founded on rigid authority, unhealthy self-deception, and a language of command a new order that incorporates greater spontaneity and creativity, one based on Cordelia's urge to speak what she felt not what she had to say.

1.3 Suggestions for a New Critical Reading of *King Lear*

A New Critic would seek in the play ironics and paradoxes that represent a successful reconciliation of contraries, a weld of universal and particular. In one of the dominant image patterns of the play, for example, two opposing values or terms are crossed. What is prized is suddenly despised, what without worth suddenly valued. The powerful and the powerless exchange places, and the virtuous are branded vicious. Both the action and the imagery of the play are characterized by such paradoxes and ironic inversions. The pattern is evident in Lear's caution to Cordelia: "Mend your speech a little, / Lest you may mar your fortunes." The two characters are close yet distant at this point in the play, joined by blood yet separated by judgment, and the trope evokes phonetic alliteration ("mend . . . mar") only to draw attention to a larger and more destructive semantic disjunction (between repairing something and tainting or destroying it). The world of words is deceptive, suggesting unity where there is actually dissonance, an irony that helps initiate the play's tragic action. In the same scene, France draws attention to the social inversion that Lear's rashness begets: "Fairest Cordelia, that art most rich, being poor, / Most choice, forsaken, and most loved, despised." These paradoxes underscore Lear's folly, that his actions toward Cordelia invert the right order of things by prizing flattery over genuine speech, false love over real, the material over the spiritual. The tropes or images themselves embody this sense of social disorder, this devaluation of valuable things and elevation of worthless ones: "We are not the first / Who with best meaning have incurred the worst."

As you pursue your own New Critical reading, you might study the play for other examples of paradox or irony. Pay particular attention to the imagery associated with sight, clothing, and madness.

1.4 A Formalist Reading of Elizabeth Bishop's "The Moose"

"The Moose" is an elegy, a kind of poem written on the occasion of someone's death that offers a way of understanding or coming to terms with death. Dedicated to Bishop's recently deceased aunt, its point of departure is a bus journey Bishop took back to New England from Nova Scotia after attending her aunt's funeral. The poem required almost two decades to compose, so its apparent simplicity belies a great deal of careful crafting. The union of simple narrative (a bus journey) and grand thematic concern (how to understand death) would appeal to a New Critic interested in the way universal meanings and concrete particulars are welded together in poetry, while a Russian Formalist would be attracted by the high degree of "literariness" evident in Bishop's crafted use of rhythm, rhyme, euphony, repetition, and metaphor.

The poem seems entirely concerned with the careful observation and precise description of ordinary events and objects, from a dog's bark to moonlight in the woods, yet this simple concern can be related to the issue of life and death on which the poem ultimately dwells. Observation and description occur at the surface where human consciousness or subjectivity encounters objective world, and that surface is also the line which distinguishes life from death, the human or subjective from the thingly or objective world. To cross that line is to move from the vivid to the inanimate. The way the poem describes objects, therefore, itself bears on the issue of death, and the form that the contact between mind and world assumes can be understood as having a thematic consequence. A fearful attitude toward death would posit the world as inanimate object. The mind's contact with the world would from this perspective be with an entirely alien realm, and the subject's passage into objectivity in death would be understood as simple extinction. Subject and object, awareness and world, thus come to have the meaning of life and death.

But it is possible to imagine the relation between life and death, subject and object, awareness and things in other ways, and that is what "The Moose" is about. The task of the elegaic poet is to conceive of death in such a way that it no longer inspires fear, and addressing that task takes the form in the poem of a journey of consciousness from an initial external perspective that observes the world in its separate objectivity to an immersion in human subjectivity that emphasizes such human powers and capacities as memory, imagination, and naming, to, finally, a vision of an object that is itself a subject and that provokes a kind of communion across the line dividing subjective awareness from the world of objects. The very simple recording of observations of natural things and everyday events in the poem is therefore also about the very human problem of how to confront one's own naturalness and objectivity, one's own final belonging to the world.

The "narrative" of the poem has four parts: the first is concerned with the movement of the bus through the landscape as seen from the outside; the second records the onset of evening; the third describes the nighttime events inside the bus from the perspective of the speaker; and finally, in part four, the moose appears. The first six stanzas of the poem consist of one lengthy sentence which begins with an unusually long introductory clause ("From narrow provinces . . .") and whose subject and verbs are "a bus journeys west" in line two of stanza five and "waits, patient" in line two of stanza six. The effect of this form is to emphasize the predominance of the landscape over the subject, the immersion of the bus in the world around it. In the unusual form of the sentence, the centrality human subjectivity usually accords itself is displaced. If the bus is a figure for humanity or for the "lone traveller" of stanza six, then already in this poem, it is portrayed as part of a world that in a profound manner precedes and exceeds it. Even when the bus finally is named as the subject, it is described in a way that emphasizes its placement within nature: the windshield reflects the sunlight, the sunlight glances off and brushes the metal, and the bus's side is called a "flank," an animal simile that foreshadows the moose and metaphorically implants the human vehicle in the natural world.

The delayed presentation of the subject also unsettles and defamiliarizes the distinction between human and natural worlds through a confusion of reference. The word "where" occurs three times in the first three stanzas as a modifier of "provinces," but stanza four begins with a clause that modifies by anticipation the bus: "on red, gravelly roads." The uninterrupted flow of reading, facilitated by the parallel of "where" clauses and the "on" clause, merges the description of the provinces with the description of the bus and further underscores the inseparability of the human and natural worlds by making the referent of "on" seem the same as that of "where." At first, one seems to be reading about provinces, and only when one reaches the next stanza does one realize that a shift has occurred and that provinces have given way to the bus as the object of the modifier.

The merged inseparability of the human and the natural is made emphatic in the use of rhythm, rhyme, and alliteration in the first four stanzas. From the "fish and bread and tea" of line two to "the bay not at home" of line twelve, Bishop characterizes nature with metaphors of human domesticity and uses the repetition of sounds to suggest the naturalness of human civilization's constructs. The civilized "roads" of stanza four, line one, are echoed in the "rows of sugar maples" in the next line, and the "ap" sound of "maples" carries over into the "clapboard" of the following two lines – the "clapboard farmhouses" which are echoed in "clapboard churches," a repetition that links human subjective concerns such as religion with work on nature. If natural woods can become literal wood for human construction, the rhyme of "churches" and "birches" intimates a more profound congruence between the two worlds.

That congruence also takes the form of a mirroring between realms. The rhythm of such parallel lines as "the bay coming in, / the bay not at home" mimes the movement of the tides coming in and going out, while qualifiers like "veins" suggest that nature's work on itself is akin to a living organism. This crossing assumes a humorous form at the end of this first part where the "collie supervises" and the bus "waits, patient."

Nature itself is characterized by a harmonic mirroring between its parts that makes the bus's journey into it – a metaphor for the passage into death – seem not so much a loss of life and a fall into cold objectivity as a move from one realm of vividness into another. The rhythmic alternation of vowel sounds in the opening stanzas, for example, suggests a nature that breathes in and out while circulating water like blood (the "silted red," "red sea," and "lavender" of stanza three). The repeated o's of line one ("From narrow provinces") alternate with a's, e's, and i's in line two ("of fish and bread and tea"), then with o's again in line three ("home of the long tides") and with e's and a's again in lines four and five ("where the bay leaves the sea / twice a day and takes"), before line six harmonically unites the three alternating sounds – "the herrings long rides."

Stanza two performs a similar alternation of sounds to match the description of water filling and emptying a bay. Now e and i sounds ("where if the river / enters or retreats") contrast with a's and o's ("in a wall of brown foam") to match the swing of the tides ("the bay coming in, / the bay not at home"). The "er" of "enters" and the "re" of "retreats" ("enters or retreats") enact the same kind of syllabic mirroring. Such mirroring, if it extends to all realms, both human and natural, implies that the harmony of the observed world balances a harmony in the human observer, and indeed the reading experience would suggest that the verbal form of the poem through these first few stanzas posits in the reader/observer a sense of orderly congruence with the world. This would explain why stanzas five and six are characterized by images of a mesh between human and natural worlds, from the "dented flank" of the bus which flashes sunlight as if it were paint to the family scene that includes the supervisory collie. If nature is domestic, so also the human is natural, and it is so in a way that is itself perfectly domestic. To be in the world is to be at home.

One might by now glean how the poem might be said to allude to the question of death even though it has yet explicitly to do so. Like the opening sentence which implants its subject within its object ("through the landscape the bus journeys" rather than "the bus journeys through the landscape"), the poem places humanity within a natural world characterized predominantly by a rhythmic alternation of movement and counter-movement. The effect of the second possible narrative pattern – the bus journeys through the landscape – would have been to privilege the activity of the subject on the object. The pattern chosen instead emphasizes the passivity of the subject as it encounters an object larger and more powerful than itself. The subject is therefore a part of something whose movements anticipate its own. That those movements consist of an alternation of contrasting elements ("coming in," "not at home") suggest that the death figuratively alluded to in the bus's westward journey will not be conceivable in any way other than as an alternation, rhythmic and necessary, with a counter-movement that forms a complete strophe akin to the poem's alternating vocalic patterns. One effect of the form of the poem, therefore, is to imply without stating a way of understanding death that fulfills elegiac expectations. It will be understood as part of natural life.

If the natural world of part one is accommodating, even comforting in its domesticity and vocalic harmony, in part two, which begins with the line "Goodbye to the elms," that world begins to disappear in the fading light of evening, and its disappearance gives rise to images of instability, the loss of attachment, and solitariness. Warmth ("burning rivulets") gives way to cold ("cold round crystals"), and the primary red of the first part is replaced by gray or displaced into the solitary point of a red light swimming through the dark. Awareness now withdraws from the world of external objects and those objects themselves begin to close in upon themselves, withdrawing from view. If the disembodied perspectiveless voice of part one is able to provide a grand vision of nature, of harmonic natural movements, and of the human community with/in nature, the perspective of the traveler in part two takes the form of partial impressions of things going past: "On the left, a red light / swims through the dark." The mind's awareness becomes fragmentary ("A pale flickering. Gone."), and the objects in the world become less connected to each other and to humans: "Two rubber boots show, /

illuminated, solemn. / A dog gives one bark." The boots indicate the absence of the person who wears them, much as the world itself now seems evacuated of that human or domestic content that had characterized it in part one. Night is a kind of death, an enactment of the dying out of light and of the world of objects it illuminates that would occur at death. The first part's communion of human and world, indicated by the link of church, farmhouse, and land, comes to a conclusion, a conclusion suggested by the image of the woman shaking a tablecloth "out after supper." In the place of contact with natural things are now the signs or names that humans append to things – "Then the Economies – / Lower, Middle, Upper; / Five Islands, Five Houses."

Images suggestive of death and of the fragility of human contact with the world come to dominate, but Bishop carefully maintains a certain faith in the naturalness of such changes, in an underlying holding together of things that withstands the falling apart that occurs at the level of perception, and in the possibility of finding alternative kinds of sustenance. That the onset of evening is initially characterized in positive natural imagery – "The light / grows richer," "the sweet peas cling / to their wet white string" – places the withdrawal of light and the loss of the world within the framework of the natural rhythms described in part one, and the continued use of images such as "lupins like apostles," which compares the rows of upright flowers to paintings of rows of apostles, continues the link of nature and religion. Moreover, the instability of perception is balanced by an image of a more profound holding together of things: "An iron bridge trembles / and a loose plank rattles / but doesn't give way."

In the stanza that follows the negative images of the loss of the world and the instability of perception – the lone red light in the dark, the solemn empty books, the dog's single bark – a compensatory image of an elderly woman bearing sustenance in the form of two market bags who gets aboard the bus and announces affirmatively that it is "a grand night. Yes, sir" further balances and rectifies the negativity of the oncoming night. Her request for a ticket "all the way to Boston" is a metaphor of continuity that seems to resolve the discontinuity of the flickering perceptions in the preceding stanzas. The last line – "She regards us amicably" – shifts the focus of the poem away from the lone subject's unstable perceptions of the external object world and toward a more social subjectivity. A first person pronoun – "us" – is used for the first time, and part three, which begins "Moonlight as we enter," will be concerned with human subjective powers and how they might be used to come to terms with the kind of loss described in the move from the first to the second parts of the poem.

Already one senses in the amicable encounter between the elderly woman and the passengers that those powers and their work will have to do with the ability of speech to make communities between otherwise isolated human subjects and to transform the world through acts of naming like "a grand night." If the woman's greeting creates an "us," a community out of different passengers and "lone travellers," language in the following stanza is shown transforming the negative nighttime world into something more positive through a creation of similitude: "the New Brunswick woods, / hairy, scratchy, splintery; / moonlight and mist / caught in them like lamb's wool / on bushes in a pasture." With the shift from daylight to moonlight, the poem shifts from a concern with the fragile perception of objects to a concern with the internal subjective power of the imagination, its ability to substitute images for things and to posit similitude between different things. Fragile objects can be replaced by more enduring images, just as the loneliness of a world of objects that pass and disappear can be alleviated by the company and benevolence of others. In this instance, the image is particularly important because it embodies the poem's ambivalence (a New Critic might say its irony or paradox) regarding the compensations for loss it proposes. "Lamb's wool" suggests literal physical warmth, but lamb also refers to the Christian tradition of religious symbolism to which Bishop has alluded at least twice already in the poem, since lamb is an image associated with Jesus. Lamb also, of course, suggests fresh life or birth, and that meaning seems more in keeping with the other transformations at work at this point of the poem. Splintery woods, for example, are supplanted by "pasture," something which, like the old woman's two bags of groceries, provides sustenance.

After this transformation of disturbing objects into comforting images, something like rest is possible for the travelers. The troubled instability of the perception of external objects gives way to an "hallucination," a "divagation" or wandering from the awareness of objects. The fragmented temporality of the trip through space is replaced by a different temporality "in Eternity" that allows the past – grandparents' voices overheard in childhood – to enter the present, so that memory and perception mix. Freed from the limitations of perception, the mind can engage different powers – memory and imagination – that allow a healing understanding – "things cleared up finally," "half groan, half acceptance" – of the kinds of losses one experiences as one travels through nature and time. If the bus journey is a metaphor for the inevitability of loss, of the passage of things and of people into the past of the ongoing journey, memory and imagination allow that past to be retrieved so that a conversation heard "back in the bus" can also be "an old conversation," one that recalls other conversations throughout life – "Talking the way they talked / in the old featherbed, / peacefully, / on and on."

Rhythm now returns to the poem, an alternation of sound and phrase in the tallying of life's losses and gains that mirrors the earlier alternating rhythm of nature: "what he said, what she said, / who got pensioned; / deaths deaths and sicknesses; / the year he remarried; / the year (something) happened. / . . . He took to drink. Yes. / She went to the bad." Unlike the use of rhythm in the description of nature in part one, however, the use of rhythm here seems to struggle against disordered contingency of events and to be at odds with what it names. Life in the conversation does not follow nature's alternating form, entering and retreating, coming in and going out according to a logic that draws forth a matching language. Language must struggle now to meet (or miss) what it names ("the year (something) happened"), and although the elements of the earlier vocalic and syllabic rhythms are there (the i's of "She died in childbirth" alternating with the o's of "That was the son lost / when the schooner foundered"), the two events are disjoined, unmatched, and only contingently related. Life's experiences cannot be like nature and cannot have the same kind of compelling and necessary alternating rhythm. They are strophic in that they alternate good and bad, but all together they comprise a list rather than a living unity, a series of accidents rather than anything with internal coherence. If the coherence of nature's movements evoked religious images, from the churches like birches to the lupins like apostles, now religion is put in question as an option for dealing with the alogical hazards, pains, and losses of life: "When Amos began to pray / even in the store and / finally the family had / to put him away." The deliberately clumsy use of "and" and "had" as end words renders formally the inappropriateness of the events described, but it might also be construed as suggesting that religion itself is nonsynchronic with the events of life.

Life's losses are unamenable to the kind of rhythm used to describe nature, and a different strategy of naming and describing is required, one that relies on poetic repetition to match the sheer redundancy of the events: "what he said, what she said," "deaths deaths," "the year he remarried; / the year (something) happened," "He took . . . She went . . ." No logic or coherence or rhythmic unity can be found in events that simply repeat without strophic alternation of movement and counter-movement. Instead, repetition functions to emphasize the seeming endlessness of loss: "the year . . . the year . . ."

But repetition might also make possible affirmative acceptance. This possibility is clear in the line: "'Yes . . .' that peculiar / affirmative. 'Yes . . .'" The first step in such acceptance is to recognize and affirm the events, to say "yes" to them rather than to turn away in fear. The kind of religious meaning evoked by the story of Amos (the name is biblical) would arrest the repetitiveness of the events and give them a meaning that would make them cease repeating. With such an alternative discarded, one must instead not only affirm losses, but also greet and affirm them again and again. The pain of the events is not something that happens once and is finished; it is so identical with life – figured again in the bus journey as something in constant ongoing movement – that it occurs repetitively. For there to be life is for there to be such repetitive ongoing losses. Any affirmation, acceptance, and understanding of them must therefore itself assume the form of a repetition. The grandparents' "yes" must therefore be repeated: "'Yes . . .' that peculiar / affirmative. 'Yes . . .'"

Repetition in the affirmative understanding of life's losses cannot have the form of the full strophed, alternating rhythm of the description of nature, but the repetition of understanding nevertheless gives rise to a kind of rhythm. By repeatedly affirming loss, the grandparents' act of understanding creates a mirroring and a rhythm akin to that of the opening stanzas: "A sharp, indrawn breath, / half groan, half acceptance." Repetition is endurance, and endurance means learning to accommodate what might be entirely alien to the subject's mode of observation and understanding. It is to repeat it, though in slightly different form, from "half groan" to "half acceptance." By being taken in in this way ("indrawn"), the object loses its cold objectivity and becomes subjective. By moving to the side of animation, loss and death enter awareness and become animate.

The poem's process of simple description now displays its full importance. It is the way (perhaps the only way) of fulfilling the elegaic task of coming to terms with death. Or as Bishop herself puts it with appropriate simplicity: "'Life's like that. / We know *it* (also death).'" The statement embodies the way affirmative description works by repeating the object in the subject's terms, by finding some familiar and similar term of comparison ("like"). Here, however, the term of comparison is life itself, a different moment of life of which what one is understanding is a repetition. Repetition, life's repetition of itself, thus creates familiarity and similarity: "Life's like that." It is something, to use the terms of part one, with which one can feel at home because "we" already know it.

The full capacity of repetition to promote a therapeutic understanding is rendered in the repetition of life by death: "We know *it* (also death)." To know life is necessarily, by the poetic logic of the apposition, to know death. But one consequence of the acceptance and affirmation described in this part of the poem is that death is now something appended and made parenthetical in relation to life. If life is a journey of observation and description and, through observation and description, affirmation, then all one can know is observable life. Death is known only as what stands outside life (in parentheses) and as what stands in strophic, rhythmic balance with it. By italicizing "it," Bishop underscores the rhythm and directs the reader not to place the emphasis on "know." The stress therefore falls in the middle of the line, creating a flow upward that then descends downward and back up again into "death": "We know *it* (also death)." Repetition here assumes the form of rhythm. The painful repetitiveness of loss, by being repeated in the mind's own language of observation and affirmation, is transformed into strophic, rhythmically alternating, harmonic form.

The sense that death has been understood and accepted is underscored by the comparison of the grandparents' talk to "the way they talked / in the old featherbed, / peacefully, on and on." Such talk is ongoing, itself a repetition that promises more repetition, endurance that takes its model from past acts of endurance. The poem now also returns to (repeats) the earlier image of the dog who accompanies humans on their journey ("down in the kitchen, the dog / tucked in her shawl"). The dog wrapped in a human shawl is a figure of the nonhuman accommodated to human forms of understanding and life. The loss of awareness, of life, that would be death, can now be construed as something other than the becoming blank object of the human subject. It need not have the meaning it seemed about to have in part two, that of the loss of the world in which one is immersed. The acceptance of loss fittingly now coincides with an acceptance of the loss of awareness: "Now, it's all right now / even to fall asleep / just as on all those nights." Repetition allows one to conceive of the loss of consciousness as something familiar ("just as on all those nights"), and it permits one to understand and accept the departure of any observable moment ("Now") as something which implies a repetition of a similar moment ("now"). Because of the ongoing repetition of now's, one can let go of consciousness, of the token of one's subjective life, without fear of loss. As rhythm seemed to hold things together in part one, here at the end of part three, repetition has become a mode of assurance, a promise that things will hold together, be repeated. Like the bridge that does not give way, it sustains the subject in the passage through the loss of the awareness which betokens life.

If the loss of awareness in sleep can be construed as a metaphor for death, then the appearance of the moose, which follows immediately, might be understood as itself having something to do with the issue of death. If the bus's journey has been a figure for human life moving through the world, that movement now is arrested, "stops with a jolt." Lights, those tokens of the artificial illumination cast by human civilization, are turned off, and the road of the human journey is blocked. We are in confrontation, direct and unmediated, with nature – "A moose has come out of / the impenetrable wood / and stands there, looms, rather, / in the middle of the road." The surprise is that nature, which up till now has been a landscape without subjectivity, appears as a subject, an animal which "approaches," itself the agent of the encounter, and "sniffs at / the bus's hot hood" as if it were greeting another animal. The line that divides human from natural, subjective awareness from object, life from death, is crossed in a way that confounds by reversing the distinction.

If the moose is nature understood as the possibility of the death of human life and human awareness, it is an especially harmless version of such nature. Though "Towering" or grand, it is nonetheless "antlerless," "high as a church, / homely as a house / (or, safe as houses)." It is so harmless because it is so familiar. The series of similes compare it to such comforting human institutions as a church and a house, and to the safest commercial investments ("safe as houses"). The similes cross nature and civilization and draw what might have been completely other and alien into the realm of human understanding. Life understood as the possibility of death can be understood, which is to say, taken in to familiar human terms, made comparable to what most assures us we are out of danger. By listing the passengers' reactions to the moose, the following stanza draws attention to the therapeutic power of the vision of nature as fellow subject, and the rhyme of "passengers" and "creatures" underscores the crossing of realms. The rhyme of "childishly, softly" and "It's a she!" evokes the common human and animal processes of maternity and nurturing.

The moose is now described as "Taking her time," like the grandparents speaking "in Eternity," and as looking "the bus over." Of the many continuities between the third and the fourth parts of the poem, one of the most important is the sense of being outside the limits and constraints of time, especially the time of the bus journey which brings as many losses in the passage of things as it brings gains in achieving a destination. The moose returns the passengers to childhood, just as the grandparents' voices returns the speaker of the poem to memories of voices overheard at night in her own childhood. Time loses the form of passage and becomes instead an elastic medium in which one can retrieve the lost past.

Moments of revelation when the ordinary limits of life are lifted and something else becomes possible – a vision of a different order of being – are generally associated with a suspension of ordinary time, and the revelatory, atemporal quality of this experience is suggested by Bishop's choice of the words "grand, otherworldly" to characterize the moose. Throughout the poem, Bishop has anchored the possibility of such otherworldly understanding or revelation within the everyday and the observable. Even as she capitalizes "Eternity," she keeps it tied to the actual voices of grandparents tallying and remembering and trying to understand the "Eternity" or repetitiveness of human pain and loss. She does the same thing here by anchoring the suggestion of otherworldliness, of an understanding of the moose as a symbol of something that transcends human life in perhaps a religious sense, within the passengers' reactions to it: "Why, why do we feel / (we all feel) this sweet / sensation of joy?" If there is revelation, something "otherworldly" that one can glimpse in this world, she seems to suggest, its significance resides in the feelings it generates. That those feelings are ones of joy can be understood both literally and metaphorically, as the pleasure of an encounter with an animal in the middle of the night or the realization that nature is vivid, the world warm and alive rather than cold and alien, a fellow subject rather than an entirely other object that represents the danger of the loss of subjective life.

That the most metaphoric or symbolic meanings seem difficult to extricate from the most mundane and everyday is, of course, part of Bishop's strategy in the poem. The moose is at once "awful plain" and "grand, otherworldly" for good reason. Like death in parentheses that indicate it can't be known, what spiritual or religious meaning that might exist on the other ("otherworldly") side of the moose cannot be known. Life as depicted in the poem is awareness, observation, description, and naming, and any therapeutic understanding that the poem might offer in the vision of the moose must remain within this realm; it is all there is.

Appropriately, it is to the mechanics of description and naming that the speaker now turns: "'Curious creatures,' / says our quiet driver, / rolling his *r*'s." In the euphonic repetition of c and ur sounds, Bishop draws attention to what she herself has been doing throughout the poem – supplying sound equivalents of objects in the world, describing what is primitive and primal about human life – the endlessness of life and of death – in rhythmic euphonic terms that might allow them to be understood as inspiring patient affirmation, if not occasional joy. In her own way, with the driver, she says: "'Look at that, would you.'" The passage through life need not be one of lonely observation; in euphonic language, it can be brought to an affirmative understanding.

The brevity of such moments is suggested by the succeeding lines: "Then he shifts gears. / For a moment longer, / by craning backward, / the moose can be seen . . ." If the moose is to be understood in a New Critical sense as an incarnated universal, a glimpse of spiritual life within earthly life, Bishop nonetheless underscores its dependence on earthly things – the shifting gears, the macadam, the acrid smell of gasoline that seems if anything to emphasize the worldliness of the experience. Moreover, the work of rhythm and repetition in language – "a dim / smell of moose, an acrid / smell of gasoline" – emphasizes the inextricable mingling of the otherworldly and the worldly, the vision and the eyes that see (or, in a spirit of more emphatic worldliness, the nose that smells). The rhythmic flow and counterflow – a dim smell, an acrid smell – is once again of natural things and human constructs, this time more in insurmountable counterpoint to each other, but it is also of life in its essence glimpsed and everything literal, everyday, and mundane about life that means that such vision will never be pure. All metaphors have a vehicle that, like the bus, bears its meaning, and even at its most metaphoric, its most suggestive of the possible glimpse of otherworldly meaning in life, "The Moose" reminds us of our literal placement in this world. By comparing her rather humdrum and everyday vision of the moose in the road to an older religious interpretive framework ("high as a church"), Bishop notes the kinship between her way of understanding and that older one, but like the bus and the moose, it is a kinship with a difference. Both offer therapeutic consolation for loss, one by positing a spiritual world beyond this one, hers by affirmatively looking at this world and finding in it cause (albeit momentary) for joy.

A New Critic would place greater emphasis on a possible religious meaning and see in the moose a vision of spiritual life manifesting or incarnating itself in this life. The form or texture of the poem should be understood as embodying the universal meaning that death and loss are compensated for by the "other world" that the moose symbolizes. The paradox of the poem is that the simplest things bear the grandest meanings. By putting aside great themes and concentrating on the humdrum concerns of humankind, the poem paradoxically gains access to the very world of universal meaning it seemed to be avoiding by eschewing doctrinal religion. Moreover, the New Critic would argue, by focusing on "deaths deaths" and losses, we lose a sense of what life is really about. Only by turning off the lights of the bus, a symbol of the putting aside of earthly eyes, do we gain a vision akin to religious insight ("high as a church").

A Russian Formalist reading would, like my own, be more interested in the mechanics of the poem, the way, for example, Bishop uses rhythm and repetition to achieve her goals. It would also note how the poem ruptures expectations and defamiliarizes our rote understandings by mixing descriptive vocabularies ("fish and bread and tea," for example) and by using odd syntactic structures (the long inverted opening sentence). The point of this reading would be to say that the meaning is an effect of the form, that what Bishop has to say about life and death has much to do with how she works with phonetic repetition. Such repetition provides a mechanism for coming to terms with life and death, for finding security in what might ordinarily inspire fear.

1.5   Suggestions for a Formalist Reading of Elizabeth Bishop's "At the Fishhouses"

The poem resembles "The Moose" in several respects: it begins with simple description and ends with a meditation on universal concerns; it takes place at the boundary between human awareness and nature; and it includes a suggestive encounter with an animal. A Russian Formalist would be interested in the fact that Bishop once again uses the alternation and repetition of sounds to create certain effects or to make certain points. You might read the first twelve lines again, paying attention to the way she alternates vowel sounds as she did in "The Moose" and thinking about what some of the effects created by this use of sound are. Look especially at how the man netting is described in the first six lines. Notice how she describes the world of the fishhouses and pay attention to the adjectives she uses as well as the kinds of objects she chooses to describe.

Like "The Moose," this poem can be said to be about what it means to live in the world, to be human in nature, to be a subject amongst objects. The comparison with the seal is suggestive of this theme, and the playful evocation of his "better judgment" points to the one significant difference between humans and animals, and that is consciousness, an issue that is taken up again in the last lines of the poem. You might consider how the question of knowledge bears on the metaphor of "total immersion" that applies both to the speaker and to the seal.

A New Critic would pay attention to the religious metaphors in the poem – the capstan like a cross that is stained with blood, the Baptist hymns, the Christmas trees, and the "transmutation of fire," which recalls the Christian mystical ideal of the merger of the individual soul with the soul of God once the earthly body is left behind. The New Critic would argue that the poem concerns some irony or paradox regarding the relation between spirit and matter or soul and body, and such a reading would imply that the poem concerns transcendence in some way. Consider the poem from this position and try to determine if it is organized as such a paradox.

Brooks' reading of Wordsworth in "The Language of Paradox" suggests that the irony of his poetry is that simple people could gain access to eternity in nature by seeming not to know or be aware. His reading of "The Canonization" in the same essay implies a similar theme of transcendence: bodily life conceals eternal life. The counter-argument to the idea of transcendence is that time and the world go on and on in an eternal repetition; no end occurs where bodily life changes into spiritual life. The surface of the world is all there is and all we know; no spirit stands behind it. Look again at those moments where Bishop uses repetition – "Cold dark deep," "I have seen it over and over," "above the stones," and "flowing, and flown." Consider her use of repetition in relation to the issue of transcendence. Do you think she would agree with the New Critical position?

CHAPTER 2

Structuralism

2.1 Introduction

The Russian Formalists were well on their way to becoming Structuralists when their movement was brought to an end by the Soviet authorities in the 1920s. Scientists in the realm of the literary, they studied the properties of literature in order to determine what it is and how it works. That scientific impulse was carried further in the middle of the twentieth century by a group of thinkers called Structuralists, some of whom were influenced by Roman Jakobson, one of the original Russian Formalists. Structuralists applied the insights of linguistics to literature and culture. They claimed that, like language which is both everyday speech and the language system underlying it, literature consists of a manifest level and a latent level. The latent level of the system of language consists of the vocabulary of possible terms (nouns or verbs, for example) and the rules for selecting and combining those terms which make everyday speech possible. Literature consists of manifest works like novels and poems, and it also has a latent systematic level which consists of those sets of possible terms, such as characters or images, and those rules or grammars, such as the form of the epic or the tragic plot, which determine how those terms shall be selected and combined in a way consistent with other fictions and poems. Like different spoken sentences, therefore, which manifest the same grammatical rules and have similar underlying structures, different literary works will be characterized by the same grammatical logic and possess the same invariant structure. Much as verbs always follow subjects and sometimes take objects, actions in fiction obey similar rules of consistency. Vladimir Propp, who wrote in the wake of the Formalists in the 1920s, studied Russian fairy tales and found that they shared a common narrative morphology or skeleton. Though each one was concerned with a different set of events and characters, all share the same basic set of abstract plot elements, from "The hero leaves home" to "The hero is tested in battle." Later Structuralists found that such narrative structures – the string of functions or actions linked together to form a whole story – are common to all fiction.

The origin of Structuralism is usually located in the work of Swiss linguist Ferdinand de Saussure (*Course in General Linguistics*, 1916). Saussure distinguished between two dimensions of language – how it is practiced or spoken (what he called *parole* or speech) and the language system taken as a whole (what he called *langue* or language). Saussure uses the word "synchronic" to name this systematic dimension of language; "diachronic" is his name for the historical or temporal dimension of language, how it exists and changes over time as it is spoken or practiced.

Saussure isolated the study of language as a structured system of interrelated parts from the world of objects that words name. Language, rather than a collection of names for objects, is an autonomous system of signs whose relation to objects is entirely arbitrary. Signification occurs not as a link between words and things but as the association of signifiers (sound images) and signifieds (concepts). Signifiers are constituted through their relations with other signifiers within the linguistic system and not by their relations to objects.

Two axes define the relations between signifiers: the paradigmatic, which names the vertical pole of possible substitute terms usable at any given place in a sentence, and the syntagmatic, which names the way individual elements are combined in contiguous chains to form meaningful sentences. A paradigm set would consist of a group of nouns such as cat, horse, and dog that can all fill the subject position in a sentence such as "the cat fell asleep." Each noun could substitute for the other. A syntagm would consist of any one part of the sentence that can be isolated from another, with the subject "the cat" and the predicate "fell asleep" being the two major syntagms in the example sentence. Later Structuralist linguists like Troubetzkoy noted that signifiers are constituted through binary oppositions, so that a phoneme is either voiced or nonvoiced and so on.

Saussure's ideas influenced literary and cultural criticism in several ways. They permitted Structuralist critics to shift attention away from the relation between texts and world or between texts and meaning and toward the study of literary systematicity – how texts operate logically or systematically, what the mechanisms are that produce meaning, what structures texts possess in themselves and in common with other texts, how they are made up of parts in relation to one another, and the like. A character in a Shakespeare play would be considered important from a Structuralist perspective not because he or she refers to a particular kind of person with certain human qualities. Rather, the character would be considered a part in a textual system in which that character's function is determined by its relations to the other functional parts of the system. Goneril and Regan's duplicitousness in *King Lear*, for example is a plot move that is linked logically to Cordelia's function or plot move, which might be called fidelity or restoration. Each element of the structure or system acquires meaning or significance from its relations to other parts of the system.

Saussure's ideas also allowed critics to study texts as systems of signs. Traditional humanist criticism discussed characters as if they embodied real moral qualities. *King Lear* from such a perspective would be said to be about good and evil, and the characters would be categorized accordingly. A Structuralist would instead consider the characters to be signifiers linked to signified concepts. Edmund in this light would be described as a signifier of betrayal of trust. He is as much a sign as an imaginary person, and what he signifies has meaning only in relation to other signifiers (Edgar, for example, who signifies the keeping of trust). Edmund would also be understood in terms of the signifiers that allow him to be coded negatively, signifiers of skeptical rationalism, for example, or of social mobility ("fashion fit"). Characters like Edgar and Cordelia, in contrast, are coded positively through signifiers connoting religious faith ("O dear Father, / It is thy business that I go about").

Finally, Saussurean linguistics allowed Structuralist criticism to heed the way the elements of the manifest text are combined according to latent logical or grammatical rules that are often the same as those found in other similar texts. Unlike traditional genre criticism, which would understand a play like *Lear* as depicting a man with a tragic fault who falls from grace and is ultimately redeemed by the love and devotion of others and by his own acknowledgment of wrong-doing, Structuralist criticism would seek to understand the logic of the plot, the way it is structured by grammatical rules similar to those of language. Moral qualities like innocence would be recharacterized in the binary oppositional terms of linguistics as "possessing knowledge" or "not possessing knowledge." And actions like betrayal would be placed in serial relation to other actions so that their sentential logic might become clearer. Thus, Edgar and Lear would be described as not possessing knowledge, while those who betray them – Goneril, Regan, and Edmund – would be described as possessing knowledge. In this way, a conceptual logic begins to emerge that explains how the plot evolves. The predicate "betrayal" follows logically from the state of not possessing knowledge. Treacherous actions can be taken against those who do not possess knowledge by those who do possess knowledge. The traditional way of describing the conclusion of the play as Lear's redemption would be recharacterized as a logical plot move from the state of not possessing knowledge to the state of possessing knowledge.

We can either understand a play like *Lear* as a series of snapshots of imaginarily real events that provide moral instruction, or we can be conscious that we are looking at constructed images by paying attention to the mechanics of the snapshots, noticing how their elements are chosen and arranged, heeding the logic that determines their sequence, studying the pictorial qualities of the images used, and the like. If literature, as Coleridge claimed, requires a willing suspension of disbelief, Structuralist criticism requires a willing suspension of belief, a putting aside of that primary effect of any work of literature, which is our enlistment in its illusion or in its evocative language. Literature under such scrutiny ceases to work, but precisely what makes it work becomes by that very token more available for study.

2.2 A Structuralist Reading of *King Lear*

A Structuralist critic would be interested in the fact that *King Lear* has a double plot and that the two plots are parallel though also isomorphic. That is, while Lear in the first plot moves from a position of power to loss, ultimate restoration, and death, Edgar in the second plot moves from a position of powerlessness to loss, ultimate restoration, and placement in a position of power. Despite this significant difference, the two characters can also be understood as occupying the same function in the narrative and in the meaning system of the play. Each has the qualities the play assigns kings ("a royal nobleness"), although Lear is clearly deficient in this regard, and each is posed against characters who represent contrary qualities such as "non-nobility." In the first plot, Lear serves as king until his death, while Edgar, whose actions have assured the restoration of the proper king, takes his place when the second plot merges with the first plot. The function of the dual plot structure thus becomes evident: because the play is about the succession of one king by another, the king who has faults must be shown to die, while another character, who has no faults or who through the action of the play overcomes the fault he shares with the king – both are easily duped by treacherous characters – becomes the new king. The binary oppositions that make up the meaning system of the play function to sort out the proper or right king from the improper or wrong by distributing attributes that will be the signs of kingship or of nonkingship.

Let's begin by describing the structure of the two plots. The Lear plot begins by identifying Lear with power, in particular the power to differentiate between his children by dividing his kingdom amongst them. The opening dialogue, however, is characterized by indifference. Gloucester and Kent cannot tell how the king will differentiate between two possible successors, Cornwall or Albany. In a parallel manner, Gloucester says his feelings prevent him from differentiating between Edmund, his illegitimate son, and Edgar, his legitimate son. As fathers, Gloucester and Lear are functionally equivalent, and Gloucester's refusal to honor the supremacy of the "order of law" over feeling transfers by virtue of that equivalence to Lear. And in fact, in the dowry scene which follows, Lear allows feelings to subvert the order of customary law governing marriages by refusing to dower Cordelia. The structural equivalence between Gloucester and Lear also establishes a relation of contrariety between the two, however, in that Gloucester's indifferent affection for both sons regardless of legal status contrasts with Lear's "unnatural" disregard of filial affection in his different treatment of Cordelia.

This opening move in the Lear plot from indifference to differentiation (Lear's act of dividing his kingdom) serves the function of defining a major attribute of royal power: the right to control succession in kingdoms by distinguishing the deserving from the undeserving, the rightful successors from the wrong ones. Rightful succession should flow not only to members of the royal family but also to those possessed of nobility, and when Lear confuses false speech and flattery with such nobility, he fails to perform his kingly function of distinguishing noble successors from ignoble ones. The initial plot move from indifference to differentiation thus also serves the function of indicating a danger – that indifference (the failure to differentiate among contending successors) might overwhelm differentiation. Succession might not occur properly. That Lear fails to differentiate properly indicates that he is a faulty king associated with danger within the play's system of meaning and value. Moreover, when he does differentiate by singling out Cordelia for dispossession, he places himself on the side of the treacherous characters by betraying filial attachment. He acts against "nature," the very ground of succession in royal families.

Why might dangerous indifference and faulty differentiation be presented as proximate evils in the play? The answer resides in the task the play's meaning system is meant to address: the need to find a solution to a problem of royal succession in a society which defines succession in family terms. Children normally succeed fathers as kings, but succession should also be from one noble to another, from one person possessed naturally of royal qualities to another. The problem the play addresses is of children who are not naturally noble, of characters who fulfill one imperative of rightful succession by being descendants of the king but who fail to satisfy the criterion of natural or innate nobility. The need for the second Gloucester plot now becomes evident: because Lear's children are incapable of succession (the noble Cordelia is banished and the remaining are not noble), another successor must be found, one who may not be a family member but who does satisfy the criterion of natural nobility. The purpose of the Gloucester plot is to provide a successor from outside the royal family. The dual narrative structure thus serves a major function in the play, which is to justify a move from the family as the basis of succession to nobility as the basis of succession. Goneril and Regan, the treacherous daughters of Lear, satisfy the first criterion but not the second, while Edgar satisfies the second without qualifying for the first.

The meaning system of the play works to justify the shift from family to nobility through structural equivalence. As Gloucester is made parallel to Lear both as a father and as an object of treachery, so Edgar is made parallel to Cordelia as rightful heir and as object of unjust banishment. That Cordelia is presented from the outset as distinct from others in her natural nobility thus prepares the way, at least structurally, for Edgar to acquire a similar noble characterization. Moreover, the parallel plots place Edgar in the same position as Cordelia in regard to the solution of the Lear plot, which is the one most concerned with proper succession. As Cordelia invades England from France in order to restore her father to his proper position in the family, Edgar metaphorically invades the enemy camp to challenge Edmund and to manifest the "royal nobleness" that will assure that he will be chosen as Lear's successor by Albany. By defeating Edmund, who has just admitted that he intends to assume power in the kingdom, succeed Lear to the throne, and legitimize his acts by marrying one of Lear's daughters, Edgar both overthrows the improper successor to the king and assures that nobility rather than family is the proper criterion of succession. That his legitimacy is posed against Edmund's illegitimacy further underscores the supremacy of nobility over family, since a family can contain both noble and ignoble heirs.

The play's meaning system also licenses the displacement of family by nobility as the preeminent criterion of succession in the way that nature is characterized. It operates both as the quality defining family relations – the ties of blood that bind heir to father – and as the quality defining nobility – the royal nobleness that Edgar possesses. Indeed, it is nature's indifference, its ability to generate two quite opposed things – both noble and ignoble character traits at once, for example, in the same family – that allows natural nobility to ultimately seem more important than natural family relations.

Whereas family is characterized by indifference (Gloucester's contention that Edmund and Edgar are the same), nobility is characterized precisely by differentiation (Kent's line to Oswald that he will teach him "differences," which is to say the difference between noble and non-noble).

The equivalence of indifferent nature with the confusion of the order of lawful succession in the family is evident in the opening dialogue, where Gloucester alludes to the nature of sexuality in describing Edmund and Edgar as not different from one another. Edmund, in the opening speech of 1.2, also characterizes nature as at odds with the "plague of custom" which differentiates legitimate from illegitimate. If nature licenses Edmund's treachery, it is because it is the basis of family ties that to his mind should be more important than the customary law of social distinction and proper aristocratic succession. In his eyes, nature is against the institution of legitimate succession because it does not differentiate between children.

Nature thus understood constitutes a danger to right succession. As Goneril and Regan prove, natural children can behave quite unnaturally; royal family bonds and an absence of nobility can coexist. Although by nature the daughters should succeed their father, they are not noble and therefore do not qualify. Because of the danger of indifference in the nature that defines family as a criterion of succession, another meaning of nature must be summoned in the play, and that is nature understood as innate noble qualities. Nature in this sense is difference, the difference between those possessed of nobility and those without that natural quality. Immediately after Edgar is characterized by Albany as possessing a "royal nobleness," Edmund says he will go against his "own nature" by doing something noble. Gloucester's family, like Lear's family, is capable of containing both noble and non-noble natural offspring, and because of this, natural nobility, the play argues, should be more important than the family in determining succession.

The system of meaning in the play is thus quite logical and can be said to be constructed as an argument. An initial equivalence of indifference with danger that provokes loss is ultimately replaced by another equivalence of differentiation with safety and the restoration of what was lost. The play's structure is made up of parallel parts – the two plots – in isomorphic relation to one another because both parts are required to make a whole argument, the structure of which is as follows: if a failure to differentiate leads to a loss of power, differentiation leads to a restoration of power. The middle term in the argument is nature, which is both indifferent and the grounds for differentiation.

2.3 Suggestions for a Structuralist Reading of "The Aspern Papers"

A Structuralist would consider the tale as a system. It is a narrative made up of logically connected parts, and it is an arrangement of functionally interrelated characters and themes. You might map out the system of the text, concentrating on narrative logic, character relations, and thematic elements. You might consider how the characters represent opposed values or qualities. The narrator and Juliana hold quite different conceptions of art, for example. Study their interactions to determine how they might be said to be opposed to one another in other ways. Think especially about romantic passion. You might also analyze the narrative using Propp's morphology. How might the tale be seen as a version of the fairy tale Propp describes?

A Structuralist would also notice how signs work in the tale. You might begin with the narrator and notice how textual signs indicate what kind of person he is. Consider especially James' use of signs of detective fiction and of tourism, as well of military conquest. Compare these with the signs used to characterize Juliana's house and her life. The narrator's first visit to the house is interesting to study from this perspective.

The tale is about duplicity, but it might also be said to be about the difficulty of communication between people who rely on different semiotic codes. Tina and the narrator's discussion of the papers in the end is among the more striking examples. For her, they signify a bargaining chip. For him, they signify something of much greater worth. Find other examples of the way communication in signs is fraught with misunderstanding and misinterpretation. You might consider the narrator and Juliana's debate regarding the portrait of Aspern and the narrator's thoughts regarding how the signs of romance he has made to Tina might be misinterpreted.

Finally, how might the Aspern papers themselves be understood from a Structuralist perspective? They are linked structurally to the theme of aging and death (Juliana), as well as to several motifs having to do with the irretrievability of the past – the romance between Aspern and Juliana, America when it was young, Venice before crowds of tourists came, etc. The fact that the narrator never gains access to the papers would in this light seem important. Try to connect this issue to the tale's system of meaning, especially to the oppositions that define Juliana and the narrator's difference from each other. What do the papers signify for her and what do they signify for him, and why given this might James want to make certain that the tale ends with him not possessing them? How is the ending grammatical or logical?

2.4   Suggestions for a Structuralist Reading of Elizabeth Bishop's "The Map"

The very title of this poem suggests that it will concern how we represent the world. It might also be said to be about what Structural linguistics calls the arbitrariness of the sign, the fact that words are shaped and determined less by their relationship to objects than by their relations with other words. Bishop seems to ask in this poem: if the relationship between words and things is arbitrary, then what if any is the relationship between words and things? The poem was written well before Structuralism became a well-known movement, so Bishop is not explicitly engaging Saussure or Lévi-Strauss, although as a reader of Lévi-Strauss she was no doubt aware that thinkers in several disciplines were concerned with the relationship between language and objects in the middle of the twentieth century. You might read the poem with these questions in mind and notice how she uses the metaphor of the map to draw attention to our taken-for-granted assumptions regarding the appending of words to things.

CHAPTER 3

Psychoanalysis

3.1 Introduction

Psychoanalysis studies the oftentimes skewed ways in which the mind expresses feelings. Those feelings range from anxiety and fear to hostility and sexual desire, and they can originate in a range of sources, from the traumas of personal history to the instincts of the body. Psychoanalysis is also concerned with the dynamics of interpersonal relations and with the way the self is formed through interactions with its familial and sociocultural environment. Depending on the school of psychoanalysis one heeds, the study of the mind's operations in literature should be concerned either with the unconscious and the instincts or with the family, personal history, and the social world that shapes the self.

The Freudian approach assumes that the mind has two components – consciousness and the unconscious. The unconscious is the site of sexual instincts and of desires and feelings that are considered unacceptable by the conscious mind. They must consequently be resisted, defended against, and banished into the unconscious. The instincts constantly strive toward satisfaction or release, however, and they must ultimately find some kind of expression, however indirect or skewed. Similarly, repressed desires possess an energy that moves them toward conscious representation regardless of how successfully repressed in their original troubling form. The struggle between unconscious instincts and desires on the one hand and the force of repression exercised by the ego on the other results in the displacement and distortion of unconscious contents as they strive for expression. They consequently gain representation in neurotic symptoms or in dreams instead of in more direct forms.

The conflict between the conscious ego and the unconscious instincts provokes the illness known as neurosis. Neurosis occurs when anxieties regarding unconscious feelings or instincts so overpower the ego that symptoms form – obsessional or compulsive behavior, for example, such as a fear of animals. The ego seeks to defend itself against unconscious feelings by denying them, or by converting them into their opposite, or by acting them out in indirect ways, or splitting them into good and bad components. A fear of animals might, for example, represent an inversion of a repressed sexual desire for the father. Or feelings of hostility that cannot be expressed might be turned into their opposite, and the child might perform obsessional rituals of care toward a hated parent, rituals that give no pleasure because they deny actual feelings. In neurosis, the mind still has a relationship with reality, but in psychosis the unconscious takes over altogether and expresses itself directly. Projecting onto the world, the psychotic mind replaces reality with fantastic embodiments of unconscious fears and desires.

After World War II, Freudianism was increasingly displaced by object relations theory, which rejected the instinctual basis of mental life and focused instead on the way relations between parents and children during the development process shape the self. Primary emphasis is given in much of this theory to the relations between mother and child, largely because the mother traditionally served as primary caretaker but also because the relation to the mother's body is the initial experience for all children.

If Freudianism emphasized the expression of unconscious material, object relations theory emphasizes the internalization of relations to others as a formative force that creates the self. An initial symbiotic relationship with parents evolves into relations of mature independence from them, and this occurs through the development of a sense of object constancy, an ability to live in a stable world of objects to which one relates without anxieties about separation or fusion. Object constancy results from the mind's ability to construct mental representations of objects such that the self can endure their absence. Once the child has a stable image of a primary caregiver, he or she can tolerate separation from the caregiver more easily and develop an autonomous self.

Separation is fraught with anxiety, however, and it is around such issues that neurotic behavior forms. Unsatisfactory early relations might lead to traumas that provoke feelings of terror around separation or anxieties about fusion with others. Consistent care is required to provide a sense of object constancy, and if that fails, the child experiences a narcissistic wound, a sense of a basic fault in existence that prevents the development of a stable object world. Regressive longing, splitting into good and bad objects, ambivalence, fantasies of persecution or abandonment, and desires for the reparation of wounds or the restoration of lost objects characterize psychopathology in object relations theory. Pathology tends to move either toward excessive desires for fusion or toward highly rigidified needs for separation in response to fears of engulfment.

The need to establish boundaries between oneself and others is a crucial issue in object relations theory. As the ego forms out of internalized mental representations of others, those others cease to be experienced as part of one's diffuse self and instead separate into recognizable objects. That separation institutes a boundary between self and other, the feeling that one is a separate being which is not threatened by either abandonment or engulfment. Some theorists focus on the affective dimension of boundaries – the capacity for intimacy, for example – while others emphasize the cognitive quality of mental representations, whether they are simple and oppositional or complex and differentiated. The ability to make representations is one way to posit objects that are separate from the subject, and language is an essential tool in this process.

Freudianism has enjoyed a resurgence in recent decades largely as a result of the work of Jacques Lacan. The enormous appeal of Lacan's work has to do in part with his emphasis on language. Children, according to Lacan, begin with an imaginary sense of self-identity, the "mirror stage," formed largely through an identification with an external image of themselves that is provided by the mother's mirroring attention. Everyone's self-identity is, therefore, according to Lacan, split internally, formed from a duality – a constitutive dialectic of self and other – that can never be bridged or unified. We are constitutively alienated from ourselves even as we experience ourselves as most whole.

As children mature, the separation of self from objects (and from the primary maternal object) occurs through language and the ability to name objects as separate from the self. The presence of the word or signifier indicates the absence of the thing; hence, to learn language and to enter the realm of cultural signification is to learn to make do without direct contact with the object named or signified. Particularly crucial in this regard, of course, is the primary maternal object, conceived both as the mother's body and as her mirroring attention. The initial imaginary sense of oneness with the mother is succeeded by entry into that network of signifiers which Lacan calls the Symbolic Order of one's culture and society, that repertoire of names, roles, identities, and rules that delineate who we are and how we shall behave. From that point forward, all desire is conditioned by that initial sense of having lost a primary oneness or wholeness, of a lack that is ultimately unfulfillable. The desiring subject can only pursue a chain of signifiers that metonymically point to that lost sense of wholeness while never being able to provide anything but metaphoric or surrogate access to it, a series of part objects that never provide a real equivalent of that imaginary unity.

The original cut that separates the child from the mother inserts a word in place of a thing. One must come to realize that one can never have the mother, that the primary attachment ceases with passage out of the imaginary plenitude of self and (m)other into the Symbolic Order which institutes separation both as the line between child and mother and as the bar between signifier and signified in language. That separation consists of the recognition that access to the mother's body is denied the child, that the imaginary oneness of self and object must give way to a sense of the irreducible otherness of the object (and by implication of all desired objects throughout life), and that the signifiers that enable such separation also imply the irrevocable absence of all signifieds, their entombment in the unconscious. If the presence of the word is the absence of the thing, then to be obliged to live in language (what for Lacan entry into the Symbolic Order entails) is to learn to endure the permanent absence of objects and the impossibility of any unity with or presence of the thing named or desired (what the imaginary unity with the mother supposedly provided). With this separation from the mother, the paternal injunction against incest (the "Law of the Father") initiates the passage into the Symbolic that institutes adult self-identity as something founded on a primordial alienation that can never be healed.

Several reading strategies emerge from these psychoanalytic theories. A text might be read for the way unconscious material manifests itself through indirect means – images or descriptions that evoke psychological issues. The relations between characters might be studied for what they disclose about family dynamics and the way such dynamics shape selves. A psychoanalytic reading might also attend to such themes or issues as separation, loss, boundaries, fusion with others, and the struggle to form a coherent and functioning self out of a damaging context or a traumatic personal history. Finally, language itself can be studied as a means of instantiating unconscious processes and working through some of the issues an emerging self faces as it struggles for adult existence or as it seeks to come to terms with disturbing unconscious material.

3.2   A Psychoanalytic Reading of Elizabeth Bishop's "In the Village" and "Sestina"

A psychoanalytic reading of Bishop's poetry might take its point of departure from a prose piece entitled "In the Village" about her life in Nova Scotia during her youth. The piece describes her reactions to a visit home from a sanitarium in Boston by her mother, who is suffering from schizophrenia. The central event in the piece is her mother's scream while being fitted for a new dress, a scream that expresses the mother's terror of a world perceived to be threatening and that becomes for the child hearing it a metonym for the mother's distance from the child. That distance or absence seems to have the effect of disturbing the child's sense of boundaries between subjective interiority and objective exteriority, so that many of the child's observations are characterized by crossings – of perceptual and actual realms, of modes of being, of metaphoric qualities – similar to those that characterize Bishop's poetry (see especially "The Map").

Consider the first paragraph. "A scream, the echo of a scream," it begins, "hangs over the Nova Scotian village." The poem begins with a displacement (from scream to echo), as if the painful event had to be distanced and de-realized from the outset; it is never allowed to exist. The distancing continues through transformations and deflections that change the scream into other things while questioning its reality. "No one hears it" yet "it hangs there forever, a slight stain in those pure blue skies." Metaphoric displacement shifts the scream out of the auditory realm and into the visual ("stain"), where it ceases to penetrate the mind and becomes instead a visible and perhaps masterable object. Its pain is also reduced by its placement within "pure blue skies" that offer a calming background to the stain, a compensatory alternative of a nature that is essentially untainted or undisturbed.

The work of displacement continues along a metonymic pathway as the observations regarding the skies continue: ". . . skies that travelers compare to those of Switzerland, too dark, too blue, so that they seem to keep darkening a little more around the horizon – or is it around the rims of the eyes? – the color of the cloud of bloom on the elm trees, the violet on the field of oats; something darkening over the woods and waters as well as the sky. The scream hangs like that, unheard, in memory – in the past, in the present, and those years between." The scream unsettles boundaries between realms, between sky and fields, a crossing signified by "cloud of bloom," which is both a metaphoric crossing and a semantic crossing in that "cloud" is the literal cloud of the preceding sky, as well as a figure for the appearance of the tree's blossoms. The scream also disturbs the child's sense of the distinction between perception and thing – "or is it around the rims of the eyes?" The mother/child relation usually establishes secure boundaries or distinctions between self and world, but the scream and the disturbed relation it signifies seem in this rendering of experience to have upset that normal patterning of self and objects.

Ultimately, the scream is more powerful than the pathway of relief chosen by Bishop. It hangs "over" the sky and the woods. Its power as an occupant of her unconscious is indicated by its "unheard" quality and by the fact that it lives through time, actually in the past, yet in the present as well. Like the unconscious, it is "alive forever," and it is identical with the place of her youth and therefore with her youth itself: "Its pitch would be the pitch of my village."

The purpose of the prose piece, however, is to let the scream be heard in a way that permits something like healing to occur, and indeed, the first paragraph ends with an indication of such a direction: "Flick the lightning rod on top of the church steeple with your fingernail and you will hear it." The fantasy of a giant hand is one of empowerment and of mastery over a painful and traumatic experience. It permits the scream to be heard without fear. It is as if Bishop were urging herself forward into what remains to be written in the prose piece when she writes "and you will hear it." One way to let it be heard, of course, is poetry, and the prose piece concludes with an image of a blacksmith, a traditional metaphor for the poet, whose clanging sounds smother the scream entirely: "Oh beautiful sound, strike again!"

"The Moose" might be read in a similar fashion; it concerns a coming to terms with trauma. In this case, it is the trauma of the death of the aunt to whom the poem is dedicated, an aunt who shared a bed with the young Elizabeth and who comforted her during her mother's madness. The aunt is thus connected to the mother, and the poem might thus be said to deal with the child's earliest experiences of separation from a mother whose illness prevented her from being present to the child in the first place. The very first word of the poem – "From" – places it in movement away from something left behind. Like the echo of the scream that distances and by displacement protects, the opening gesture situates the poem at one remove, in a kind of initial echo or state of displacement. If there is nothing before displacement – with the significant exceptions of the title and the name of the dead aunt – that may be because the loss is too painful to be experienced directly.

Like "In the Village," "The Moose" rectifies trauma through metaphoric crossings, especially of nature's objectivity and human domesticity – "of fish and bread and tea, / home of the long tides / . . . the bay not at home" – that represent the cold objectivity of things in such a way that they lose their separateness. Within this framework, the moose can be read as an ideal internal object, a mental representation that compensates for what is lost in the world of objects but that also allows separation and loss to be tolerated more easily.

Bishop deals with loss in a similar manner in "Sestina." The title draws attention to the fact that the poem is a formal exercise, a following of poetic rules. Given that the occasion of the poem is an unstated but deducible emotional catastrophe, the title might also be interpreted as a defensive movement of displacement away from pain and toward activities that substitute order and control for uncontrollable distress. That one possible substitute activity might be poetry itself lends the self-referentially poetic title an added accuracy.

The first suggestion of pain or loss is the "failing light" of the first stanza, an image that recalls the troubling disappearance of visibility in "The Moose." As in that poem, domestic warmth and a grandparently voice serve as compensations, though here they fail in their task, and the child falls back on her own representational resources to deal with grief. Those resources allow her to transform and control a potentially dangerous object world by externalizing her own emotions in a playful reordering of the things around her. That work of reshaping arises out of a strong sense of separation or withdrawal of her self from the world, a separation that is signaled by the emotional geography of the stanza. "September rain" represents an external assault on the house, the origin of grief, that is balanced by the more internal "her tears." As in "The Moose," external and internal realms, objectivity and subjectivity, define a movement inward from objects to self and from perceptions associated with pain to private representations that provide substitute comfort. That movement crosses the internal and the external and is as much a symptom as a cure.

In stanzas two and three, the grandmother attempts to soothe grief by locating it within an order of prediction associated with a farmer's almanac. The tears are now "equinoctial," part of an external, seasonal order, and they with the rain are both "foretold by the almanac," something that makes them part of a predictable object world. But the crossed rain/tears are themselves symptomatic of a boundary disorder, a confusion of internal and external worlds. The predictability of the almanac protects against this liquidity or boundary fluidity, as does the grandmother's role as predicter and protector: "*It's time for tea now.*" If distress takes the form of an object world that seems to assault the self in the form of rain, producing a disruption in the relation between self and other, self and world, and provoking a confusion of boundaries, the attempt to provide comfort seeks to establish a bounded order of everyday ritual.

For all of her effort, however, the grandmother cannot succeed. A metonymic chain of displacements is at work in the poem, one associated with the form of the sestina, that shifts the terms of grief and undermines the grandmother's attempts to provide order. The external rain shifts to tears, which become "the teakettle's small hard tears," which are transformed into "buttons like tears." The form of the poem prescribes a repetition and displacement of its key words that is reflective of the way grief travels from one sign or object to another, moving away from and around an original loss that cannot be named except as "It."

That original loss has to do with the mother's failure of care, and indeed, one could say that the poem's drama of grandmother and child reenacts that failure: ". . . but the child / is watching the teakettle's small hard tears / dance like mad on the hot black stove, / the way the rain must dance on the house." "Like mad" refers to her mother's condition, the occasion for the trauma that ignites the poem, and to the uncontrollable emotions that event provokes. That uncontrollability disturbs the boundaries between things and between self and world, and that disturbance appears as a disturbance in representation. The child does not see objects; she sees metaphors – "teakettle's . . . tears," "dance like mad," "the way the rain must dance." Objects are transformed into substitute mental representations, and as a result, there is no clear sense of distinction between the child's mental processes and objects. At the same time, the breakdown of the distinction between internal and external, tears and rain (both now "dance"), becomes more pronounced in the poem. Her pain is experienced both as an external attack and an internal eruption.

But her ability to representationally transform objects might itself be a vehicle of healing. By objectifying emotions, it renders them more controllable; by internalizing objects, they become less dangerous. If the trauma originates in the failure of the primary relation between mother and child, a failure that results in a feeling that the external world of objects is dangerous and that one's own emotional reactions are uncontrollable, that failure is repaired by subjectivizing objectivity, transforming stoves and books into animate things, and by objectifying one's own dangerously uncontrollable emotional reactions in the form of representations that bring a sense of predictability and control.

The next stanza begins with an example of this process: "*It was to be*, says the Marvel Stove. / *I know what I know*, says the almanac." By projecting her own feelings into the objects, the child enlists their assistance, gaining consolation from the stove and the power of esoteric knowledge from the almanac. In the preceding stanza, the almanac is described as a quasi-maternal presence that "hovers half open above the child." It is also an emblem of representation, of writing that provides a sense of predictability. Through its "I know what I know," the child establishes the realm of her private representations as the site where recovery can be accomplished.

Stanza five contains an image of such representation. The child makes a crayon drawing of a "rigid house," an emblem of emotional rigidity and of the failure of the maternal relation. But she also begins to integrate the terms of grief to her representations – "Then the child / puts in a man with buttons like tears." That she "shows it proudly to the grandmother" suggests that the exercise is part of a process of healing the maternal relation. In stanza six, the powers of control of the almanac are integrated with her representational powers: "But secretly, while the grandmother / busies herself about the stove, / the little moons fall down like tears / from between the pages of the almanac / into the flower bed the child / has carefully placed in the front of the house." Moons, emblems of an imagination or power of representation that works in the absence of daytime empirical perception, blend with a figure of creative rebeginning. The loss of objects can be accepted because the work of representation can transform a dangerous object world into images that stand in front of the rigid house and compensate for its deficiencies.

In the final half stanza, "*Time to plant tears*" suggests the burying of grief as well as its appropriation to a process of repair. If the confusion of boundaries between private representations and objects is a symptom of disturbance, it can also, when done "carefully," be the means to a cure. Appropriately, the grandmother, that stand-in for the mother, is now enlivened and made celebratory. She "sings to the marvelous stove," another object transformation – from Marvel stove to marvelous – made possible by language. Like "The Moose," this poem ends on a dual note of a recovered maternal care made available by one's own powers of representation to cross objective and subjective realms and of a reconciliation to distance and separation: "and the child draws another inscrutable house." The house is at once the absent mother, the child's art of repetitive representation, and the inscrutability of a private world of feeling that remains unconscious and successfully defended against, the invisible basement of the house of art and the foundation upon which it is built.

The Lacanian description of the figural character of desire and repression is clearly pertinent to the poem. "Tears," the signifiers of pain or loss, not only travel through the formal equation of the sestina, they also are mobile in a transformative psychological sense. Initially a displacement of the rain that figures the external cause of the child's suffering, the tears are domesticated into tea, and eventually into water for a garden in front of a crayon house, an imaginary externalization that completes the circuit of suffering, grief, and recovery. At each step of that metonymic journey of displacements, the figure of pain is repeated and simultaneously made different. This is the therapeutic magic of the form of the sestina, which allows for metamorphosis and stasis at the same time, a compulsive repetitive reenactment of pain that slowly diminishes its power and reduces it to comedy. In this way, a symptom of trauma becomes a vehicle of reparation.

3.3   A Psychoanalytic Reading of *The Bluest Eye*

My brother-in-law is a psychiatrist at a major US urban university hospital. It is a city with a large poor black population whose history can be traced back to the post-slavery migrations north in search of employment. The city was long ago abandoned by whites, and with them went the wealth that might have provided sustaining employment for the black population. In the absence of such employment and of the secure community and family structures it makes possible, the black population suffers from all the usual disfigurements that poverty breeds, including a higher than normal incidence of mental illness. In the emergency room at the hospital, my brother-in-law sees people with visions, people bent on killing themselves, people who talk endlessly to no one, people suffering from paranoid delusions, people so out of control they have to be tied to beds, and so on. After several years of such work, he concluded that mental illness is not a randomly occurring event strewn across the city population, an occasional statistically predictable dysfunction in a population enjoying the usual rate of normal mental functionality; rather, it is so widespread that it is almost more congruent with the experience of urban poverty than the usual psychological model of normality.

I tell the story because it draws attention to the need for social psychoanalytic accounts of certain kinds of mental illness. It also speaks to the world portrayed by Toni Morrison in *The Bluest Eye*, a world of intense poverty in which traumas to the self that breed mental illness take the form of events with social as much as personal origins.

The opening of the novel describes a world of desire that might appear familiar to a Freudian psychoanalytic critic: "Nuns go by as quiet as lust, and drunken men and sober eyes sing in the lobby of the Greek hotel." Like a dream, the image juxtaposes incongruent things – nuns and lust, drunkenness and sobriety, quietness and singing – and foreshadows how the novel will contain a number of instances of the mixing and confounding of things that should be kept apart: a father's lust and a daughter's vulnerability, a mother's job as caregiver for white children and her rejection of her own children, marriage and mutual hatred. By placing nuns and lust on the same plane, the image suggests that what the nuns represent – religious ideals connected to the control of sexual impulses – are not able in this world to overwhelm the power of lust, and by joining drunkenness and sober eyes, it suggests that the social traumas that generate pathologies like alcoholism also produce eyes that see the world without illusion and are, as Morrison will put it later in the book, dangerously free of a sense of care for others.

While the image might be said to stage emblematically the currents flowing into Cholly Breedlove's rape of Pecola, it also points out the way the personal and the social hinge with each other.

The opening paragraph is also about desire and its blockage, though what is desired is inflected by social determinants like poverty and ethnicity, and the blockage has less to do with internal psychological censors than with social and material obstacles. Rosemary Villanucci, who is white, sits in her father's relatively new automobile, a 1939 Buick, "eating bread and butter," an object desired by Claudia and Frieda, two black girls. In a gesture of racial and class exclusion, Rosemary tells them they can't come into the car, and the experience of exclusion, combined with that of material deprivation and hunger, produce anger and fantasies of revenge in Claudia: "We stare at her, wanting her bread, but more than that wanting to poke the arrogance out of her eyes and smash the pride of ownership that curls her chewing mouth." Desire and denial are in this situation interpersonal and dynamic, and the flows of willfully mean or destructive energy are inaugurated by extrapersonal determinants such as ethnic group antagonisms that dictate from sites beyond the individual will or unconscious how a white girl will aggress and a black girl respond. Such chromatically coded lines of conflicted social encounter seem distant from Freudian erotocentrism and are characterized more by dynamically determined feelings of shame and pride. Yet when Rosemary offers to pull her pants down as a token of submission that will help her avoid a beating, and out of pride, Claudia refuses, one finds evidence of the use of a vocabulary of sexual submissiveness in negotiating even social antagonisms that seem purely economic and ethnic in character. What the novel asks is that we heed both the way sexuality provides a vocabulary for interaction across the lines dividing social groups and the way sexuality is scripted elsewhere, in the battered personal histories and broken lives that are direct effects of economic dispossession and material deprivation.

As in psychoanalysis, which requires that one read what is evident to the senses for what it conceals and deflects, Morrison's novel moves from the proscenium of pain and pathology to the background of social causality. After describing the painful encounter with the white girl, she moves on to give an account of Claudia's world. The girls live near a steel mill, and as they watch the red hot slag being poured down a ravine at night, they feel the cold of the dead grass against their feet. The image suggests the alienation and distance of blacks from the white-dominated economic world where great heat is expended in making the goods of modern industry, even as those left out are obliged to scrounge for leftover pieces of coal to heat their frigid houses. The coldness of Claudia's world is also a metaphor for parent/child relations that barely nurture or provide sustenance: "Our house is old, cold, and green. . . . Adults do not talk to us – they give us directions. They issue orders without providing information. When we trip and fall down they glance at us; if we cut or bruise ourselves, they ask us are we crazy. When we catch colds, they shake their heads in disgust at our lack of consideration. How, they ask us, do you expect anybody to get anything done if you are all sick?" It is a world in which the stress of poverty rivets the adults' attention on such basic issues of survival as how to heat a house in winter so much that they cannot provide the care and attention that children need. Claudia describes the effect of such neglect on children: "Our illness is treated with contempt, foul Black Draught, and castor oil that blunts our minds." Claudia's description evidences the swerving of consciousness away from trauma, in this case, the painful experience of the failure of parental care. That failure to provide disturbs the child's sense of a clear boundary between self and object, internal and external world. Boundary lines weaken and normally discrete realms cross and merge. In Claudia's description, "illness is treated with contempt," a psychological disposition, but it is also "treated" in a medicinal sense with "Black Draught." The very progress of these opening paragraphs evidences a similar disturbance of spatial boundaries and of a sense of temporal continuity, as Claudia moves from an event on the street, to a story of picking scrap coal outside at night, to a description of life inside her home with callous parents, to a story of her being ill, to expressions of doubt about the veracity of what she recalls: "But was it really like that? As painful as I remember?" The instability of parental care translates into an uncertainty about oneself and one's experiences.

Yet for all her callousness, Claudia's mother is for her someone "who does not want me to die." When Claudia's cough was "dry and tough," her mother would pad into her room in the middle of the night to adjust her quilt and make her comfortable. And always behind the mother is the broken window whose crack lets cold air in: " 'Get some rags and stuff that window.' . . . The rags have fallen from the window crack, and the air is cold. . . . Love, thick and dark as Alaga syrup, eased up into that cracked window." Poverty makes Claudia and her family vulnerable to the cold in a number of senses. Literally, it is figured in the broken window that must be stuffed with rags because the family cannot afford to have it fixed. But the window is also a metaphor for being vulnerable to a cold external world whose racism and economic exclusiveness propels blacks into stressful poverty that places pressure on family relations, relations that might otherwise be more sustaining and nurturing.

The novel thus opens by establishing a close link between personal trauma and social conditions. The lack of food, money, shelter, and comfort scars the self and engenders feelings of anger, resentment, humiliation, and uncertainty. In such situations, healthy psychological development is threatened if not impossible. Morrison devotes the rest of the novel to describing the kinds of pathological behavior such negative social and economic environments provoke. In doing so, she carefully links environment to personal history.

Given her concern for portraying environments that do anything but breed love, Morrison's choice of "Breedlove" for the family that will be most emblematic of poverty-induced trauma in her novel can only be understood as ironic. It is appropriate that our first encounter with them is a parentless child, Pecola, who comes to share a bed with Claudia and her sister Frieda. Pecola is defined as a character by her yearning. She drinks large quantities of milk, as if compensating for an absent maternal care, and her question regarding her new physical powers of reproduction – "how do you get somebody to love you?" – suggests just how deprived of affection, nurturance, and care her home life has been. Given these deficits, Pecola's desire to be entirely other than herself is understandable. She has been treated in such a way as to diminish her sense of self-importance, and she therefore locates an object of identification in a blue-eyed white doll. Her desire for blue eyes is a response to an uncaring and unproviding environment. It resembles Claudia's swerve of consciousness away from traumatic pain that crosses illogically from one realm to another. If the logic of reality is such that it induces pain, then that logic and that reality must be tricked and undone by the mind if it is to survive the experience of pain.

A black girl's desire for a white girl's blue eyes is one way of countering the painful realist logic that would have black girls be permanently excluded from the world of public praise that accrues to whiteness. What happens to dolls – that the white ones are praised and the black ones don't exist – is also what happens to girls: Pecola's mother turns her out in order to care for the white girl for whose parents she works. The desire for blue eyes is in effect a desire for care, for the care and nurturance that is given to others. This desire, because it runs counter to the logic that defines how care will be distributed between economically secure families and economically insecure ones, can only result in madness, since for Pecola to expect care of the kind that financially secure white children experience contradicts the governing rationality of the world in which she lives. The logic of reality that defines her environment, her family, and her experience of life as deprived also places her expectations outside any conceivable rationality. The unreason of madness is a figure for a desire that seeks to break the link between environment and self, impoverished social context and damaged care.

The Breedloves are first presented in relation to a specifically economic environment that is so powerful it becomes equated with home ("There is an abandoned store . . ."), and Morrison devotes a great deal of care to the delineation of their personal histories. In their regard, she reinvokes the metaphor of heat – a stove that sees fit to fail every morning – to describe the family's failure both as a functioning social community and as a source of care for children. Each member of the family lives in a "cell of consciousness," an image both of fragmentation and imprisonment, that helps account for how Paula might refuse care to her own child in order to provide it for another or for how Cholly might become so obsessed with his own pleasures and impressions that he rapes his own daughter. The equivalent of the broken window in Claudia's family is a sofa with a rent in it that figures the economic mistreatment of blacks by whites and becomes an occasion of persistent joylessness which pervades everything in the family's lives.

Both Cholly and Paula fail as providers of parental care because they were each themselves victims of parental neglect. Abandoned by his own mother at birth, Cholly is raised by an aunt who dies, and when he seeks out his father, he is greeted by rejection. Paula's lame foot is a metaphor for her lack of a feeling of self-worth, and it is directly connected to the parental "indifference" that allowed the nail wound that caused her lameness to become so deadly. Paula's feelings of ugliness provoke her to seek out compensations in the world of white movie culture and white ideals of beauty. In her job as a servant for whites, she has access to a sense of order and beauty that are denied in her home life by poverty. Her rejection of her daughter is shaped and determined by this contrast. To care for her daughter would be to lose what most makes her happy and most compensates for the traumas in her own life.

Cholly is a more extreme example of the negative psychological consequences of white racism and black poverty. Because whites have more social power, his humiliation at the hands of two white men while making love to a black girl results not in feelings of anger at the whites but in feelings of anger against the girl. Like the sofa that breeds joylessness, objects linked to significant feelings define Cholly's personal history as a broken and fragmented narrative: "The pieces of Cholly's life could become coherent only in the head of a musician. . . . Only they would know how to connect the heart of a red watermelon to the asafetida bag to the muscadine to the flashlight on his behind to the fist of money to the lemonade in a Mason jar to a man called Blue . . ." Without the kind of parental nurturing and care that would have made his life a linear development of healthy psychological potentials and traits, Cholly ends up "alone with his own perceptions and appetites, and they alone interested him." No one cared for him, so he cares for no one, least of all those closest to him or most within his range, like his wife or his daughter Pecola. Because he did not experience a kind of care that would have instilled in him a coherent and consistent sense of self and of self-worth that would have allowed him to control his impulses and to map the link between impulse, action, and consequence, he is capable of pursuing impulses regardless of their consequences. Morrison describes him as made "dangerously free" by his experiences, but in the context of family relations that require a great deal of responsibility in one's actions toward others, especially in the care one gives children, such freedom easily veers into a damaging irresponsibility.

In her description of Cholly's thoughts and feelings just before the rape, Morrison fulfills the prophecy of her opening sentence, with its curious juxtapositions: "Cholly saw her dimly and could not tell what he saw or what he felt. Then he became aware that he was uncomfortable; next he felt the discomfort dissolve into pleasure. The sequence of his emotions was revulsion, guilt, pity, then love. . . . He wanted to break her neck, but tenderly. Guilt and impotence rose in a bilious duet." Staged here is not the representational ambivalence of the dream thought, but rather the emotional ambivalence that someone with Cholly's personal history is likely to experience. Deprived of a coherent sense of self and battered by humiliating and painful traumas, Cholly is overwhelmed by feelings that have no order or logic or coherence. The most opposed and contradictory impulses cohabit in his experience. His psychopathology is defined by this inability to sort out one mode of emotion from another, so that he can experience both himself and the world in a stable and coherent manner. The inability to keep contending emotions apart accounts for his inability to recognize the line of appropriate behavior that would keep his own sexual desire apart from his daughter. The line from his mental incoherence to the incoherence of the act (both morally and narratively) to the incoherence his act breeds in Pecola is direct and causative in both a narrative and a psychological sense. The failure to be loved properly results in the failure to love properly.

3.4 Suggestions for a Psychoanalytic Reading of *King Lear*

A play about madness would seem to offer ample material for a psychoanalytic study, but the normal relations between characters seem in the play to be as significant psychoanalytically as the mad scenes. Critics have noted, for example, that Lear's relations with his daughters recall the relations of a male child with its mother. They also note that real mothers are absent from the play and they ask what the significance of this absence is. You might reread the play with these issues or questions in mind. Think about how a Freudian, an object relations theorist, and a Lacanian would all describe the play differently. Each one would no doubt have a different way of accounting for Lear's madness, and each would interpret his relations with his daughters differently.

In addition, you might consider:

- the way Edmund's mother is characterized in exclusively sexual terms in the opening dialogue;
- the link between that depiction and the other topics of the opening dialogue, including the depiction of Lear as indecisive and the discussion of the distinction between legitimate and illegitimate sons and heirs;
- the imaginary quality of Lear's request for flattery from his daughters;
- the significance of Cordelia's refusal to flatter, especially given her use of the word "nothing," which is Renaissance slang for the vagina;
- the effects of the loss of Goneril and Regan's care on Lear, especially his loss of a sense of identity;
- the way in which women's sexuality is depicted in the play;
- the character of Edgar as Tom O'Bedlam and what he represents in regard to female sexuality or the "fiend";
- the violence done to sexually powerful women at the conclusion of the play.

3.5   Suggestions for a Psychoanalytic Reading of "The Aspern Papers"

A Freudian psychoanalytic critic would treat the tale as a fantasy that translates unconscious or repressed material into figural form. How might the narrator's quest for the Aspern papers be understood as an index of unconscious yearnings? You might look again at the moments when the narrator discusses his desire for the papers. Think about how the papers are characterized and with what they are associated. It might be especially important that they seem to represent for the narrator access to romantic passions he himself seems incapable of experiencing. They might thus represent a substitute for sexuality, but what does that say about the narrator's relationship to sexuality?

Note as well the role of sexual innuendo in the tale – the name Cumnor, for example, or the narrator's statement that he would not find himself in the same box (a slang word for a vagina) as Aspern. The narrator masquerades or masks his true identity and his true feelings in order to attain the object of his desire. An obvious question would be: what is he really hiding and why? What do the papers represent in an unconscious sense that makes the disguise of one's desire for them necessary?

You might relate these issues to the way the narrator enacts a mock romance with Tina. When she offers him marriage, it is in an oddly worded version of playing doctor ("You could see the things; you could use them"), and he, of course, flees. Look again at those scenes with Tina and notice the pronominal displacement as well as the temporal ellipses. They would seem to indicate anxiety, but if so, what is the anxiety about?

An object relations critic would read the tale's character relations as a family drama. The narrator's relations to Juliana and Aspern are like those of a male child to a mother and a father. Juliana seems more threatening than endearing, and you might consider why this might be the case. Think about his relations with her as those of a child and a mother and notice how the issue of boundaries enters into their interactions. Bordereau might be understood as watery boundary or border, since "eau" is French for water. How might an absence of boundaries be threatening to a male child?

The narrator idealizes Aspern and turns to him or to his portrait whenever he needs help in dealing with the female characters. Look again at those moments when the narrator thinks about Aspern. You might relate these to Freud's description of the ego ideal in his essay on narcissism.

CHAPTER 4

Marxism

4.1 Introduction

A work of literature always possesses form and structure, but it always also exists in time and space, history and society. To appeal to audiences, a literary work must speak to concerns that readers recognize as relevant to their own lives. It must have a social dimension. In addition, a literary work always bears the imprint of the historical moment in which it was written. *King Lear* is about kings, late feudal ideals, and court intrigues because it was written around 1600 when such things meant something to audiences.

The social and historical study of literature can take a number of forms, but one of the most popular in literary study is Marxism, which combines an understanding of the social roots of literature with a sense of its political ramifications. Marxism is appealing in part because of the story of human history it tells. Marx conceived of human life in its most basic terms. It is organized around the production of goods for human consumption and survival. Marx noticed that all societies are arranged in such a way that a large group of workers does the labor of production while a small group of owners reaps the benefits and accumulates wealth. All history, he contended, is characterized by such unequal class arrangements, and one result is that all history is characterized by class struggle, the conflict between those who own and those who labor. Humans imagine that great historical change is the result of their own ideas or wars of conquest, but according to Marx, economic development plays a more determining role. When agricultural overproduction made surpluses possible in the feudal economy, trade developed, and with trade came a new class of merchants who accumulated wealth, built towns, and eventually developed social and political forms more appropriate to their way of doing business and their new way of thinking, one shaped by ideals of free trade and individual liberty, as opposed to the ideals of obedience and fealty that characterized feudal society.

Such ways of thinking Marx called ideology. Ideology or "the ruling ideas of the ruling class" is a way of legitimating or justifying social and economic arrangements that might otherwise appear unjust because they are characterized by inequality. Those who rule or who possess economic power need to convince everyone else that the arrangement of the world is reasonable, or natural, or good. They also need to elicit the consent of those whose subjection to the role of productive workers is needed for the society to survive. In feudal times, ideology consisted of the belief that the ruling nobility were of a higher genetic order than mere laboring commoners, that subservient behavior in this life would be rewarded in the afterlife, and that there was a natural, theologically ordained order of rank which prescribed social roles. In modern times, ideology (in the anglophone capitalist countries at least) consists of the belief that humans are free individuals rather than social beings, and as individuals they freely strive for success in an open economy. Those who succeed do so not because initial class position determines where one ends up in life but because talent results in deserved success. Those who fail are not victims of systemic pressures that allocate rewards to the already well placed; they are simply not deserving.

The relationship between literature and ideology varies over time. In the late Renaissance when Shakespeare wrote, literature was produced in close proximity to the sites of political and economic power. The largescale segregation of spheres that characterizes modern society had yet to occur. Consequently, plays like *King Lear* depart very little from the ruling ideas of the ruling class; indeed, in one reading, the play is an overt polemic in favor of the values and ideals of the ruling aristocratic group and a denunciation of the new group of merchants and lawyers who aspired to displace the aristocracy. In modern capitalist societies, cultural production is both more autonomous from and more hostage to those with economic power who own such sites of cultural production as publishing houses and television networks. Control over cultural production guarantees that books that are critical of capitalism do not attain wide circulation. At its most autonomous, literature can take the form of James' "The Aspern Papers," a tale that ridicules the commercial spirit of modern capitalism, or of Elizabeth Bishop's poem "A Miracle for Breakfast," which criticizes the disparity between wealth and poverty during the Great Depression.

Marxist literary criticism takes two major forms. The first seeks to locate literature within its social, economic, and historical context and to understand how the ideas advanced in the work of literature relate to the ideals and values that circulated in the society of the time. Such criticism tries especially to link literature to class struggle, to the conflicts between social groups that contend for economic and political power often by cultural means. A second major form of Marxist criticism consists of a critique of ideology. It seeks to understand how ideology works in literature to mask social contradictions such as those between economic groups. Because ideology aspires to a total or universal description of the world, one which makes it appear as if the perspective of the ruling group is valid for everyone, it must make contradictory or dissident perspectives seem like temporary departures from a norm. They cannot appear to be valid perspectives in their own right that contradict the values of those who rule or who possess economic power. Nevertheless, according to Marxism, all ideology, because it masks real contradictions, contains fissures or faultlines within it where those contradictions manifest an obdurate resistance to ideological pacification. The marks of class struggle on a culture are pervasive and indelible, and they are legible in literature.

4.2 A Marxist Reading of *King Lear*

In each epoch, according to Marx, there is a fit between social relations and mode of production, but as the mode of production develops, the old social relations come into contradiction with the new economic realities and are burst asunder; new social relations must evolve that match the needs of the new economic reality. The feudal system was held together by bonds of fealty and duty; serfs were bound to lords and could not seek work elsewhere. But once trade developed, work became available in cities, and the serfs could flee the land and become wage laborers for early capitalists or apprentices for guilds. The new economic reality made new social relations possible, ones based on contract and wages rather than fealty and tribute.

According to the Marxist theory of history, feudalism contained within it a contradiction that allowed it to evolve into capitalism. The feudal economy, which was organized around agricultural labor by serfs for lords, generated surpluses that allowed trade to develop. The new class of traders and small manufacturers required new rules of social relationship (contract as opposed to fealty, for example) that more suited their economic reality. Their trading activities made it necessary for them to live together in towns rather than out in the country, where the feudal lords held sway and possessed the power to interfere with trade. The development of towns and the growing power of the merchant class allowed the development of new political forms such as the Constitution and the Republic that were more in keeping with the needs and interests of the merchants. In conjunction with the economic might of the merchants, such new political forms meant the demise of feudalism.

King Lear is situated at the juncture between the old feudal form and the emerging capitalist form of society. In the England of 1606, the emerging class of primarily urban merchants, traders, and small industrialists were already more wealthy than the neofeudal nobility, whose life of nonproductive consumption was becoming increasingly ill-suited to their own survival. The inflation of prices induced by trade and by the influx of gold from the colonies in North America was bringing financial ruin to the aristocracy, whose incomes from tenant farmer rents remained constant, while that of the merchants increased. As a result, the nobility was obliged to sell land to nonaristocrats, and a new gentry of wealthy landowners came into being. At the same time, James I, in order to gain money, sold aristocratic titles to members of the merchant class. This resulted in an "inflation of honors" and a depreciation of the value of the marks of nobility. The laws of inheritance or primogeniture, which conveyed land to the first born, also meant that many nobles found themselves with title but no land. A new group of landless nobles came into being.

England was undergoing a social and economic upheaval whose significance would not be realized until mid-century when the monarchy would be overthrown in a bloody civil war. In 1606, the new class of merchants, small industrialists, and traders was already beginning to assert itself by arguing with King James over prerogative (who should make laws) and over sustenance (the money Parliament had to pay to support the king's rather extravagant way of life). Those differences reflected deeper conflicts of value and ideology. For one thing, the new class was opposed to the idea that aristocrats deserved to rule by hereditary right and that society consisted of a fixed order of rank. They were committed to the more egalitarian ideal of individual responsibility and achievement, which held that anyone might gain wealth and rise in society. While the nobles thought noble lineage earned one the right to a leisured way of life, the new class, some of whom were Puritans, an absolutist form of Protestantism, felt that one proved one's worth through industry and frugality. The nobles supported the king's claim to a "divine right" to rule as he wished, while the new class insisted on the power of Parliament, where their own interests were best represented and where their "liberties" (and property) could be protected by law. The new class believed in dissent, the old in obedience. The attitudes of the new class were also shaped by the new scientific rationalism and empiricism of the period, which encouraged skepticism toward the old neoclassical beliefs (Ptolemy's spheres being one example) that sanctioned the aristocratic model of social order. While the aristocracy represented the residues of a society bound together by ideals of service, loyalty, and obligation, the merchant class represented the beginnings of a social form dependent more on relations of contract and consent, ideals that would serve as the basis for the new liberal constitutional theory that would eventually replace monarchism later in the seventeenth century.

The relevance of all of this to *King Lear* should be evident. It concerns a large landholding aristocrat whose loss of power is directly linked to a loss of land. All the traits and trappings of Lear's character suggest neofeudal nobility, from his arcane language ("vassal," "recreant") to his unproductive way of life based on consumption and leisure. Moreover, Lear is situated within social relations that revolve around feudal notions of duty and obligation. What he expects of his daughters is "service," and his ability to command such service is indicative of the power the feudal nobility possessed.

His downfall is an allegory of the contemporary "crisis of the aristocracy." His loss of land is representative of the way land was losing its economic power and being replaced by trade. And the disrespect he experiences suggests the decrease in deference toward the nobility from a merchant class for whom the traditional claims to obedience made little sense. The play thus depicts a threat posed to the traditional aristocratic order based on notions of privilege and obligation, by the newly emergent capitalist philosophy which favored individual ambition in the pursuit of social mobility.

The first scene of the play can be read as evoking a world of feudal forms and customs. We learn that the king is about to choose between two lesser lords and are given an image of a hierarchical power structure in which lower-ranked nobles must depend on a monarch. The exchange between Kent and Edmund introduces us to feudal forms of deference: "My services to your lordship." Edmund's remark, we learn later, is ironic, since he will betray the feudal system of social relations. The irony will prove significant because the play will depict the internal faults of the feudal world, those things like the disinherited son that threaten its existence from within.

Having established a feudal norm, the play sets about breaking it. The break occurs when feudal social relations, which are based on mutual loyalty and trust, are confronted with early capitalist relations, which are based on individual ambition, disrespect for traditional notions of duty, and distrust. The opposition between the aristocratic way of thinking and the emerging capitalist social philosophy is evident in the contending concepts of value at work in the dowry scene. From an aristocratic perspective, value is inherent or innate, while from a capitalist perspective, it is ascribed from without by market exchange; nobility is not a matter of temperament or lineage but of money. Lear's distribution of dowries, while arranged around feudal relations of mutual obligation, is tainted by market exchange. He invites his daughters to bid for land ("prize me at her worth") and gives it in exchange for expressions of love that he interprets as promises of care.

Cordelia's rebellion represents an attempt to reassert the appropriately aristocratic ideal of fealty. It should be a matter of recognized custom, not market exchange: "I love your Majesty / According to my bond, no more nor less . . . I / Return those duties back as are right fit." She draws attention to the fact that Lear breaches the aristocratic system by asking more in return than, according to custom, he deserves. That Lear's tragic fault might be economic in character is suggested by the way he characterizes Cordelia's position once he revokes her dowry. "[H]er price is fallen," he tells Burgundy. Lear thus participates in the betrayal of the traditional aristocratic mode of valuation by the new capitalist one. His declaration that "Nothing will come of nothing" implies that value is no longer inherent. If something has to come from something, market exchange, rather than inherent worth, determines value.

Cordelia might thus be understood as an emblem of how the nobility was changing in the world created by the new capitalist class. In the new social system dominated by market exchange, family bonds or lineage made little difference; instead, one's value came to depend on external valuation, or "price." Deprived of her land, Cordelia is placed on the market and subjected to external valuations. For Burgundy, she ceases to be a good bargain: "I crave no more than hath Your Highness offered, / Nor will you tender less." It falls to France to refute the principle of market exchange and reassert the aristocratic concept of value as inherent worth: "She is herself a dowry." He calls her "most rich, being poor" and an "unprized precious maid." Aristocrats are valuable in themselves – by virtue of noble birth. Even without land, they have value. Before departing with France, Cordelia offers an aristocratic characterization of the representatives of the new system of valuation: "Well may you prosper." Unlike aristocratic wealth, which is stable and land-based, the new capitalist wealth is indeed meant to prosper and grow.

As representatives of that new sensibility, Goneril and Regan break the feudal rules of reciprocal trust and personal obligation first by lying to their father, then by refusing what is his due under the feudal rules of obligation. They ignore the "[e]ffects of courtesy, dues of gratitude" that hold traditional aristocratic society together. In that society, the stability of the family and the state are closely connected, since monarchical succession is determined by family lineage, and since the power of the feudal lord, who derives from the patriarch of the clan, depends on a sense of duty comparable to family allegiance. A breach of family duty is therefore an injury to the relations of obedience that hold the state together. "Death on my state," Lear appropriately cries when his bargain is broken.

The most representative member of the new class is Edmund. He speaks of the feudal system as the "plague of custom," and he questions the customary distinctions between legitimate and illegitimate that will deprive him of property. He represents the new merchant individualism in his avidity to rise in rank. He disrespects tradition and questions aristocratic authority; his language is laced with references to trade ("I grow, I prosper"); he overturns feudal rules of succession and tries to rise illegitimately into the nobility by acquiring land and titles which do not rightfully belong to him; and he articulates a skeptical rationalist way of thinking which is critical of the religious ideology that sustains the aristocratic world ("we make guilty of our disasters the sun, the moon, and stars"). If the traditional ideology (most noticeably represented in Gloucester) portrays a world of stable hierarchies that prescribe attitudes of respect and obligation, the new rationalism, associated with the new empirical sciences which are represented negatively in the play's mathematical references ("My daughter / Thou art nought"), promotes a skeptical understanding that questions those hierarchies. It permits calculation, both in a mathematical sense and in an economic sense, since the new economics would be based on productive commercial investments, not on the consumption of already held landed wealth.

Linked to Goneril and Regan by the word "prosper," Edmund is like them associated with fabrication ("And my invention thrive . . . ," "All with me's meet that I can fashion fit"). He betrays feudal family obligations for the sake of making his own way in the world. Whereas Gloucester's aristocratic way of thinking deplores "the bond cracked twixt son and father," Edmund's new philosophy of class mobility embraces that breakdown as an opportunity: "The younger rises when the old doth fall." If the feudal system of fealty and obligation rested on assumptions of trust (without modern contracts, one had to trust another's word on agreements), the new system associated with Goneril, Regan, and Edmund is characterized by distrust. Indeed, the great danger of these characters is that they pretend to follow the customary rules based on trust, only to break them.

Opposite Edmund stands Edgar, whose reference to "Child Rowland" associates him with feudal rites of initiation (an initiate to knighthood was called a child). Indeed, he ultimately becomes the new king after luring Edmund into a feudal test of truthfulness. His actions are guided by the very feudal ideals of duty and loyalty that Edmund despises. It is fitting that Edgar aids not only the head of his own family but also the head of the social or state family, both his father and his king. He thus fulfills Gloucester's conception of the interconnection between state and family, public and personal duty. By restoring one, he restores the other. If Edmund, in keeping with the ideology of the new merchant class, acquires a noble title through artificial means, Edgar emanates natural nobility from within and eschews the signs of wealth by pretending to be a poor madman. When Albany says of him "Methought thy very gait did prophesy / A royal nobleness," he sets his nobility within the realm of religion, the meaning system that sustains the idea of natural hierarchy.

Kent is also an embodiment of appropriate feudal attitudes. He represents trust ("to serve him truly that will put me in trust"), as well as an ideal of fealty and service to his lord, whom he seeks out even after he is banished. Loyalty is in his nature, not something ascribed by his position in the division of labor: "Now, banished Kent, / If thou canst serve where thou dost stand condemned, / So may it come thy master, whom thou lov'st, / Shall find thee full of labors." In the exchange with Lear in which he pledges service, he carries out a similar exercise of naturalization on Lear himself. Lear's right to demand service does not derive from social position; rather, it is inscribed in his "countenance / which I would fain call master." This naturalization of the aristocratic division of labor accompanies a concept of social rank as something unconstructed that should evoke recognition. Thus, when Kent confronts Oswald, the emblem of the unfaithful servant, he says "I'll teach you differences," by which he means differences of rank.

The Fool, another loyal servant, chides Lear for having upset the natural order of social rank: "[F]or he's a mad yeoman that sees his son a gentleman before him." He harangues the king for having given away the land that is the basis of aristocratic social power ("so much the rent of his land comes to" – "Nothing") and repeatedly draws attention to the link between landed property and social identity: "Thou wast a pretty fellow when thou hadst no need to care for her frowning; now thou art an O without a figure . . . [T]hou art nothing." He also articulates the aristocratic critique of wealth and of opportunistic expediency of the kind associated with the values of the new merchant class: "That sir which serves and seeks for gain, / And follows but for form, / Will pack when it begins to rain."

Finally, it falls to the Fool to state the empirical equivalent of the tragic metaphor. That tragedy is as much a crisis of aristocratic privilege as it is the expression of a personal fault. Lear associates it with "revolt," and after he "commands, tends service" to no avail, he speaks of the "dues of gratitude. / Thy half o' the kingdom hast thou not forgot, / Wherein I thee endowed." Lear's is the tragedy of a transitional economy, when the old rules of obligation are no longer honored and when money and mercantile power have superseded aristocratic prerogative. When, as if in an aside, the Fool speaks of "No squire in debt, and no poor knight," he describes the contemporary equivalent of Lear's plight. It is the plight of someone with a title but without means.

The ideological work of the play consists of evoking disaster and then healing it. The disaster is identified with the triumph of capitalist values, and the rectification consists of restoring aristocratic values defeated earlier in the play. The first step in restoration is to reaccredit the grounding of the aristocratic ideology in a cosmological or natural scheme that lends it legitimacy. Albany, the figure in the treasonous camp most endowed with inner virtue, begins the process when he accuses Goneril in words that evoke the equation of social and cosmological orders: "If the heavens do not their visible spirits / Send quickly down to tame these vile offenses / . . . Humanity must perforce prey on itself." Throughout the final two acts, the idea that the Gods oversee human life, rewarding aristocratic virtue and punishing new class ambitions, is repeatedly asserted. "This shows you are above, / You justicers, that these our nether crimes / So speedily can venge!" Albany says. And later: "This judgment of the heavens, that makes us tremble, / Touches us not with pity." Even the fallen Edmund, the strongest critic of this ideology, capitulates: "'Tis true [that "The Gods are just"], / The wheel is come full circle."

Cordelia is the character most associated with ideological healing. She reestablishes the aristocratic ideal of service to one's lord (and to the aristocracy in general). Her physical healing of Lear is worded in economic and political terms: "No blown ambition doth our arms incite, / But love, dear love, and our aged father's right." If Edmund makes his own "business" central, Cordelia, evoking Christ, says of her father that "It is thy business that I go about." And her servants identify Lear as "a royal one" and offer to "obey" him.

In *King Lear*, the aristocratic world evokes a nightmare that it hopes will never happen and offers a cure that consists of affirming the need for absolute respect for custom and for absolute obedience to kings: "To him our absolute power." In the face of a rebellious merchant class and an uncontrollable market, the traditional aristocracy would increasingly in the early seventeenth century resort to absolute monarchical rule, a strategy that helps precipitate civil war. Thus, the play can be said to put on display a contradiction within monarchical pre-capitalist society. Faced with an increasingly powerful adversary, the aristocracy must resort to means of survival that only exacerbate the conflict and hasten its own demise.

Moreover, while the play depicts a crisis that justifies an absolutist solution to assure the maintenance of feudal rules of obligation, it puts in question the viability of the very feudal institutions of duty, obligation, and mutual trust that it sets out to defend. If anything, the play demonstrates why the capitalist rationalization of agreements through contracts was necessary. Lear's agreement with his daughters would not be so easily breakable if it were more contractual: "Thy half o' the kingdom hast thou not forgot, / Wherein I thee endowed . . . I gave you all – / Made you my guardians, my depositaries, / But kept a reservation." The play portrays contractual agreements negatively, but in its depiction of the untrust-worthiness of nobles themselves, it also demonstrates why contract would eventually supersede feudal notions of duty and obligation. In an old feudal world of stable wealth and fixed ranks, trust was sufficient, but in a new early capitalist world of fluctuating wealth and social mobility, something else was needed. *King Lear* condemns Edmund and associates him with both the new rationalism and the new prosperity, but it also depicts a flawed feudal set of social arrangements that cry out for the kind of rationality he represents.

While the play sides with the nobility then against the new class, it depicts precisely why the nobility would have to be superseded. They were given to resource-consuming "domestic and particular broils" and wars that would no longer be acceptable to the more frugally minded merchant class, who preferred a world of stable trading arrangements over one in which everything could be overturned in a thrice and all their hard-earned wealth expended on a war ignited by a personal quarrel between the likes of Albany and Cornwall. The play does depict those quarrels negatively. When Goneril says that "The laws are mine, not thine. / Who can arraign me for 't?," she describes a kind of legal particularism (as opposed to rational universalism) that monarchs took away from local lords and barons. Edgar's ascension in the end represents a reinstatement of that monarchical role. But monarchs were themselves given to "broils" with foreign monarchs, and the local problem of unproductive internecine conflict merely played itself out on a grander international stage. One crucial hinge of the plot, recall, is a foreign invasion. While the play defends a neofeudal aristocratic ideology, therefore, the very instrument of plot resolution – a war against rebellious barons – also depicts why that ideology (and that social system) would ultimately have to give way.

The play resolves the contradictions it depicts within the aristocratic world in spurious or imaginary ways. Edgar's ascension is magical, his pure virtue scarcely credible. Those solutions contain fractures where the intractability of the underlying contradictions manifests itself. The triumph of virtue, for example, is inseparable from a mere martial victory over adversaries. The play attempts to deprive such contradictions of their obduracy and pacify them, but the contradictions prove irresolvable in history and eventually lead to revolution. Those whose ideas fail in *King Lear* themselves eventually succeed in the field of battle. To a certain extent, the play itself, even at its most ideological, suggests why this will be the case. The contradiction in Renaissance society and culture between the emerging ideal of human liberty, promoted by the new merchant class, and the ideal of authority espoused by the traditional aristocracy, is resolved in the play by the transformation of an absolutist king into an object of pathos. By "humanizing" the king, Shakespeare welds together the two contending poles of monarchical authority and individual subjectivity or liberty that were so much at odds in his culture, but in doing so in a manner designed to reinforce monarchical absolutism, he expands the reach of subjective self-reflection, a process that can only further the erosion of customary aristocratic authority by depriving it of its automatic character. The play reflects on a structure of power that survives on the basis of nonreflective obedience, but it does so in a manner that encourages subjective reflection of a kind at odds with such submission. It should not be surprising then that kings would, in the period following the play, become increasingly absolutist. If *Lear* is a good example, the culture was becoming altogether too thoughtful to consent unreflectingly to royal rule.

4.3 Suggestions for a Marxist Reading of "The Aspern Papers"

By the late nineteenth century, the time of the writing of "The Aspern Papers," capitalism was in full flower. The merchant class, last seen struggling against superior odds in the late Renaissance of *King Lear*, was in full control not only of the major industrial countries of western Europe and North America but also of their satellite colonies throughout the rest of the world. In the twelfth century, if you wanted to see foreign lands, you had to join a Crusade. Now, if you had enough money, you could become a tourist, or if you didn't, you could join one of the new imperial European armies that were carving up the world in search of raw materials to feed the expanding industrial machines at home. It was the "age of Empire" (roughly from 1875 to 1914), and with the plundered raw materials of colonialism came enormously high levels of production, consumption, and wealth in Europe and North America. England, where Henry James wrote in voluntary exile, had been the dominant industrial power for a century and was still powerful; America, his homeland, was overtaking it, armed with a larger population, a weaker native population more readily shunted aside, vaster natural resources, and greater industrial capacity. The harnessing of huge dispossessed populations to the new industrial machinery gave rise to levels of production and consumption that transformed the world.

It was the Gilded Age – ornate, mannered, wealthy. But it was also an age of harsh exploitation for working people, a topic that occupied "realist" writers like Zola, Sinclair, and Dreiser. James chose to write about the leisure class, people with incomes that permit them to travel and educational levels that permit them to speak in a highly refined language. They are not capitalists themselves, but they benefit from and do not make much of a fuss about the human cost of wealth and leisure. Nevertheless, James is far from being an ideologue of an exploitative social system. He treats with some irony the representatives of the new commercial order, with its mail order catalogs and colored advertisements. And he uses a syntactically sophisticated language to describe complexities of feeling, thought, and social intercourse that offer a resistant counterpoint to the simplistic calculi of capitalist economics. A conservative in regard to what he sees being destroyed by the new commercial order, James is a progressive in his criticism of the monetary opportunism that carries out that destruction.

The rapacious, unfettered capitalism of the age can scarcely be said to play a major role in "The Aspern Papers," although the very fact that the novel is *not* about the evils of economic exploitation and the plight of working people – the everywhere visible downside of capitalist modernity that preoccupied many of his fellow writers – would be of significance to a Marxist critic. In James' preoccupation with the minutiae of desire in a bourgeois setting, such a critic might be tempted to find evidence of a serious abdication of social responsibility that could be attributed to James' "modernism," his concern with the intricacies of literary and narrative form at the expense of more pressing historical commitments. Yet such a critic might also be interested in the way the spirit of the age does appear in the novella, in the constant references to monetary transactions, for example, as well as in the character of the narrator, whose quest for the Aspern papers is rendered in terms that underscore its economic significance.

You might study the tale for other ways in which capitalism and capitalist values enter into the tale's story. One important issue would seem to be the relationship between commodification and art, as well as between market exchange and romance. The conflict between the narrator and Juliana is in part defined by the first relationship, while the second defines the relationship between the narrator and Tina. You might note how Juliana represents a rather different concept of value from the narrator and try to understand that difference in terms of the difference Marx describes between use value and exchange value.

4.4   Suggestions for a Marxist Reading of Elizabeth Bishop's "A Miracle for Breakfast"

Lyric poetry is a genre of private meditation rather than public commitment. The impulse in Marxism toward changing a society deemed unacceptable in its basic design would seem to place demands on lyric poetry that such poetry, with its tendency toward the personal, the smallscale, and the idiosyncratic, could never answer. There is within Marxism, however, also a strand of thought (the work of Benjamin and Marcuse particularly) that would locate in lyric poetry alternative modes of perception and description that call forth a vision of worlds at odds with a repressive reality or that draw attention to the workings (and unworkings) of ideology within the hegemonic culture. The poetic imagination may indeed deflect larger social concerns, but it may also be implicitly critical and utopian. "The Moose," for example, might be read from a Marxist perspective as offering a beneficent vision of the interpenetration of natural and social worlds that is implicitly critical of the ethics and epistemology of capitalism, which sees nature as an object to be profitably exploited.

A more explicit example of social criticism in Bishop's work can be found in "A Miracle for Breakfast," a poem written in the 1930s that evokes the bread lines of the Depression, when unemployment and homelessness made people seek free handouts of food from charitable organizations and from the government. Bishop gives added emphasis to such images of economic distress by juxtaposing them to an image of a wealthy man who is a dispenser of charity. You might study the different languages of description Bishop uses for the different participants in this social drama. She signals her attitudes toward each in her choice of adjectives and images. You should pay special attention to her use of religious images and references, from the parable of the loaves and fishes to the image of the sun (or son) walking on water.

You might also study the relationship between the first part of the poem and the last few stanzas, which contain a fantasy of a utopia in which all needs are filled as well as the suggestion that the miracle in question in the poem, which might be said to have to do with the filling of basic needs such as hunger, has already occurred. Notice how Bishop makes her political argument through her choice of images. You might also think about how that argument is made through the way the poem is organized. It is a sestina in which each stanza uses the same six concluding words (coffee, crumb, balcony, miracle, sun, and river).

4.5 Suggestions for a Marxist Reading of
The Bluest Eye

Marxist criticism is primarily concerned with economic domination and the way it shapes or is represented in literature. The workers whose exploitation Marxists study are often also specific ethnic groups, and that was strikingly the case in the southern United States before the Civil War, where Africans who had been forcibly converted into slave laborers did most of the agricultural work. During the era of slavery, the culture and family structure of the African people were systematically destroyed. They were prevented from acquiring an education or learning to read, and families were frequently broken apart and members sold to other slave owners. Women in the camps were subjected to systematic rape and obliged to bear children for their white masters.

While the slave system was abolished by the Civil War, little was subsequently done to improve the economic status of the former slaves. The era of Reconstruction immediately after the war saw some improvement in their political rights, but without property, many very quickly found themselves trapped in a new kind of economic bondage – the tenant farm system. And the gains of Reconstruction were soon turned back by a backlash of white opposition. Most political and civil rights that Africans had gained were revoked, and the US Supreme Court went so far as to sanction a system of segregation between races in the South that essentially deprived Africans of equal access to education, employment, and the political system. An informal system of harassment against Africans, whose most savage form was lynching, also was institutionalized in the South and remained in place until the 1960s, when an almost national effort was required to force its end.

Despite having their indigenous cultures and family systems destroyed, and despite centuries of enforced illiteracy, many Africans, even during the era when slavery was in force, acquired education, learned professions, and became successful in American economic life. For many, making one's way meant making one's way out of the South to the North. Immigration became a fact of African-American life, especially after agricultural mechanization in the early twentieth century forced them off their farms in the South and after new industries such as auto-making and steel-making beckoned them North. But African-Americans also fled the indignities and the brutalities of racism in the South – the constant denial of their rights of citizenship, the blocking through exclusion and segregation of their attempts to rise out of poverty, and the waves of lynching such as occurred after World War I, when over seventy blacks died in one year alone.

But racism was also prevalent amongst whites in the North, and African-

Americans once again found their efforts to advance themselves blocked by school segregation, by the denial of well-paying jobs, and by being obliged to live in poor housing in cities whose economic vitality disappeared as whites fled to segregated suburbs. Forced to remain in poverty by economic exclusion, Africans also found themselves faced increasingly with the social and cultural problems that poverty breeds – family instability, high rates of illness, drug abuse, and crime. Poverty reproduced itself by generating behavior that precluded escape through economic success.

Conservatives as a result argued that poverty was the fault of blacks themselves. Charles Murray and Richard Hernstein, the authors of *The Bell Curve*, contended that lower IQ or intelligence accounts for such pathologies as drug abuse, crime, broken families, and lack of economic success. Liberals countered that this argument takes an effect for a cause. Blacks may not score as well as whites on IQ tests because they are obliged through systematic social racism to live in poor environments, attend less well-funded schools, have lower incomes, and be victimized as a result by broken families, lower self-esteem, mental illness, higher levels of stress, and the need, induced by a negative context, for alternative palliatives like drugs. If the social and economic playing field were leveled and blacks given the same supportive material contexts as their better-scoring white competitors on IQ tests, from well-funded schools to high-income jobs, their performance, the counter-argument goes, would be equal. The difference is not genetic but economic.

African-American writers often take as their subject matter this continuing history of combined race and class oppression. Toni Morrison in *The Bluest Eye* looks at poverty from inside the lives and the minds of the poor. Written in the late 1960s and published in 1970, the book emerges out of a time when the status and place of African-Americans in American society had moved to the forefront of national attention. Since World War II, blacks had been militating for political equality and economic justice using such tactics as sit-ins and boycotts against segregated restaurants, schools, and bus systems in the South. Eventually their protests obliged the federal government to pass legislation banning discrimination.

You might reread the novel with this history in mind and think about how Morrison uses personal histories especially to tell her story. In regard to the Breedloves particularly, she seems to want readers to know where they came from and how they got to be where they are. You might think about how their life stories intersect with the larger history of blacks in America.

Notice as well how Morrison portrays the effects of poverty on the lives of black people, especially Claudia's family and the Breedloves. How are their lives shaped and determined by economic class? How does Morrison suggest their lives might have been different if it had not been for poverty?

CHAPTER 5

Post-Structuralism, Deconstruction, Post-Modernism

5.1 Introduction

In the 1960s, Structuralism, which had dominated French intellectual life since the mid-1950s, began to be replaced by another more antinomian movement that eventually would be called first Post-Structuralism, then Post-Modernism. If Structuralism emphasizes order, structure, and rules, Post-Structuralism argues that language is subject to contingency, indeterminacy, and the generation of multiple meanings, that reason, rather than being an instrument of understanding, is instead an instrument of mastery, discipline, and social control, and that all the values, ideals, and norms of western philosophy and western social life – from truth conceived as a clear idea present to the conscious mind to the individual conceived as a free agent who determines his or her own destiny – deny the materiality and contingency of existence, which is characterized by movement, change, and multiplicity, rather than logic, regularity, and identity.

The ramifications for literary criticism of this intellectual change-over were profound. The Structuralist desire to describe the invariant structures of literature gave way to the Post-Structuralist emphasis on those dimensions of language, psychology, and social life which undermine precisely those stable orders of meaning, identity, and truth that Structuralism seeks to establish. Post-Structuralist critics would be more concerned with the contingencies of identity, the undecidability of meaning, and the indeterminacy of the world.

Inseparable from the radical politics of 1968, the year students and workers rose up in protest against the French state and almost overthrew the government, Post-Structuralism itself represents a radical dismantling of some of the most important assumptions underlying western culture and philosophy. Paramount among those assumptions are the belief that reason provides access to a realm of pure ideation which transcends matter and language and that in such a supra-sensible realm reasoning proceeds without assistance from signification, which is derivative and secondary in relation to thought. Such a model of ideation provides an authoritative standard for truth conceived as the presence of the idea or concept in the mind, a standard that sustains and is sustained by such traditional western value oppositions as the soul and the body, culture and nature, spirit and matter, etc. Truth and ideation thus conceived allow reason and rationality to be categorically opposed to its others – madness, nonsense, nontruth, falseness, representation, metaphor, imitation, artifice, etc. – by an apparently clean cut that disjoins logic from rhetoric or speculative philosophy from mere grammar. A related assumption of such metaphysics is that the natural and social sciences describe a world of objective facts; they are not discourses that construct schematic orders of power/knowledge out of a flux of experience.

The Post-Structuralists connect these philosophic and scientific assumptions to the way society and the self have been conceived in the west. Western social life is supposedly rational and civilized, but Post-Structuralists argue it is disciplinary and carceral. The ordering power of reason merely allows a moralistic segregation of well-disciplined and functionally useful "good citizens" from dissident troublemakers. Similarly, the individual self or subject, the basis for the western political ideal of liberty and the capitalist ideal of freedom, is defined by his supposed conscious awareness and his ability to control his own destiny. Post-Structuralists argue that he is an effect of unconscious psychological processes, society-wide systems of symbolic construction, and cultural discourses that are beyond "his" control. Moreover, in western thought, the regnant system of Oedipalized heterosexual family relations charged with engendering sexed subjects is conceived as being a normalizing institution, rather than a machine for constraining and compressing a potential multiplicity of desires, possible identities, sexual object choices, and libidinal energies into more easily manageable, compartmentalized and limited identitarian forms.

Further, the Post-Structuralists argue that western assumptions about what is good, true, and normal are essentially, rather than accidentally, related to patriarchalism, heterosexism, and capitalism. Moral good does not reside in what is authentic, original, and subtracted from imitation and artifice. The true and the good are the effects of processes of differentiation and replication that confound all moral identities and all simple ontologies of substance that might serve as grounds for moral systems which privilege authenticity and virtue over contingency and artifice. Finally, according to the Post-Structuralists, what we take to be real does not exist prior to simulation; rather, it is simulated into being and lent a semblance of ontological reality by virtue of acts of representation, masquerade, and posturing that are themselves more prior, fundamental, generative (of the real). Reality is the successful repression of these processes.

At stake, essentially, is everything we take to be true, how we think, and what we unquestioningly assume must be the case about thought and the world if we are to continue lending western rationalist culture our assent and voluntary participation – our institutions for producing good citizens and good monosexual boys and girls, our habits of thinking we are above matter or nature, our values based on the easy segregation of truth from signification or artifice, etc. Literature is a small part of all of this, but in as much as literature draws attention to such things as the construction of realities through signification and explores the undersides of social life that normality banishes from view (one thinks here of the mad scenes in *King Lear*), literature can be an important site for exploring the processes that Post-Structuralism claims are at work in western thinking, society, and culture, processes that must be otherwise violently suppressed if the dominant concepts of normality and of reality are to be sustained.

One common root of Post-Structuralist theory and practice is the work of German nineteenth-century philosopher Friedrich Nietzsche. Nietzsche took issue with the dominant assumptions of western philosophy and Christian idealist culture: the idea that there is a coherent human subject, the belief that reality is a stable field of objects capable of being known by a neutral instrument called reason, the belief that knowledge is a recording device rather than a machine for constructing order and identity where there is none, the idea that moral good consists of the suppression of our material natures, the belief that truth is a spiritual quality that rises above language, etc. According to Nietzsche, these concepts of truth are falsifications incapable of grasping the flux of matter and sensation in which the human subject is immersed. They ignore the way reason produces knowledge by ascribing identity to flows and processes that are differential rather than identitarian. Nietzsche discredits the moral ideals of western society, which train people to be ashamed of bodies and of the world of matter in general. He argues that material life should be celebrated, not denied. He sees all the ideals of western bourgeois society, from aesthetic beauty to legal justice, as projections of power, a will to dominate by imposing schematizing identitarian models of truth on material realities that are in flux and have no stable identity. The universal in Nietzsche's eyes is merely the dominant.

He argues that we should not ascribe meaning to the world and thereby impress upon it our desire to be unique, to stand above matter, to feel our lives made significant by a spurious notion of spiritual meaning or nonmaterial ideation. Rather, we should conceive of the world as a material process that includes human reason, as an ongoing repetition of the same – life replicating itself over and over again, endlessly – that has no teleology or finality or goal such as a spiritual afterlife, as matter without meaning.

Nietzsche's critique of western moral idealism continues in the twentieth century in the work of Georges Bataille, a French thinker whose work spans the era from the mid-1930s to the early 1960s and who also was a major influence on Post-Structuralism. Bataille argues that western society and culture represses materiality and heterogeneity in favor of a homogeneous stasis based on rational utility and human servility. Humans project closed systems of thought and morality on the world and seek to expel everything that discloses the human link to materiality, such as sexuality, excrement, and death. Capitalism organizes life around usefulness and appropriation, while ignoring what is most rich about life – expenditure without reserve, the pure enjoyment of pleasurable excitation without any conception of its utility. The sacred is one experience that is a metaphor for our attempt to reconnect with the material totality of nature; another more direct route is eroticism. Bataille was influenced by anthropology, especially the work on gift-giving in primitive societies by Marcel Mauss which allowed Bataille to formulate an alternative to the utilitarian exchange system of modern capitalism, an alternative in which giving away, unreserved spending without expectation of return, would replace utility.

Several ideas from Bataille reemerge in Post-Structuralist work. One is the easily transgressible limit between material nature and human life. The imagery of madness is populated by animals because we humans are still animal "in nature." Another theme is the heterogeneity, expenditure, and waste that accompanies and undermines all human rational systems that seek to be homogeneous. This excess in life must be restrained if a culture of repression and an economy of limited utility is to operate successfully. This notion applies also to language, since an excess of possible meanings must be repressed if logic and reason are to use it successfully to establish meaning and truth. Another theme is the fascination with evil, criminality, and marginality. Those branded as "perverts" by so-called normal society (writers like the Marquis de Sade) are frequently, according to Bataille, explorers of the limits between nature and culture, the appropriative and the excremental, the homogeneous and the heterological. They undermine the moral values and ideals upon which repressively normative culture is founded and draw attention to the violence inherent in those ideals of normality (de Sade's corrupt priests and ministers).

The earliest work that departed from the rage for order characteristic of Structuralism was Michel Foucault's examination of the history of madness in the early 1960s. Reason, according to Foucault, is positioned as the centerpiece of western philosophy in the seventeenth century, and that positioning requires the banishment of alternate modes of thought, which are deemed mad or unreasonable. Foucault was the first to argue, following Nietzsche, that reason is not the transparent instrument of knowledge philosophers and scientists have claimed it is, nor is it a touchstone for determining value (what is good is what is rational, for example, which is to say, good is what behaves in a certain logical and orderly way). Reason, rather, represents a certain political choice regarding what shall count as reasonable.

In later works, Foucault argues that knowledge in society consists of discourses that as much posit and create objects to be known as record preexisting realities. The way knowledge is organized in the discourses of western society is allied with the organization of power in society. Power seeps into the pores of society rather than occupying a single-state site; over time, power becomes part of the habitual everyday procedures and operations of such social institutions as the school, the hospital, the prison, and the workplace. Citizens learn to absorb and perform discipline themselves. Morality, all the various ways in which one is instructed to be "good," becomes inseparable from voluntary compliance. One no longer needs to be told what to do because one does it oneself automatically.

In the mid-1960s, the writers and critics around the journal *Tel Quel*, many of whom, like Jacques Derrida and Julia Kristeva, would become important Post-Structuralist thinkers, began to link the study of signification to radical political critiques of western capitalist society, especially to the disordering and subversion of the reigning modes for constructing subjectivity and reality through language. They focused on the way the signifying potential of language exceeded the semantic orders (the way the meaning or truth of being, of the self, of the good, etc. is established) that lay at the basis of western capitalist culture. Influenced by recent translations of the Russian Formalists and the Prague Linguists (a group with connections through Roman Jakobson to the Formalists), who emphasized the autonomy of the operations of language from meaning as well as the role of such structuring principles as binary opposition in the formation of semantic content, the *Tel Quel* writers explored the way the signifying potential of language, its ability to generate multiple meaning effects in a proliferation of possible references, posed a rich and creative counterpoint to the urge on the part of traditional western philosophy and criticism to pin down meaning into singular terms, to annul the play of language by arresting it and elevating language into a vertical structure that placed meaning over language, truth above signification. Truth and meaning are effects of signification, not the other way around, the *telquellistes* contended.

Jacques Derrida's three books of 1967 – *Of Grammatology*, *Writing and Difference*, and *Speech and Phenomenon* – provide the crucial analytic devices and concepts for much of the later Post-Structuralist critiques carried out by such thinkers as Jean Baudrillard, Luce Irigaray, and Jean-François Lyotard. Derrida, whose work is known as deconstruction, argues that western philosophy claims to speak for reason, truth, and knowledge, but that in fact it consists of violent acts of opposition and hierarchization, value judgments that unjustifiably subordinate one set of terms and privilege another. The valued terms are truth (defined as the presence of ideas or of objects in the mind), reason, rationality, meaning, logic, authenticity, originality, speech, immediacy, the living, identity, etc. The devalued terms are difference, signification, nonidentity, repetition, substitution, writing, imitation, representation, artifice, metaphor, etc. All of the first terms allow western philosophy to organize itself as a project of knowledge that seeks to determine truth in an authoritative manner by dispelling falseness. Truth must itself be untouched by falseness, by all of the devalued terms listed above, from repetition and difference to imitation and signification. Yet, to seal off truth from all of its others, to determine it authoritatively as something self-identical, proper, unique, present, vivid, and original, as something untainted by substitution, repetition, difference, and the rest, philosophy must rely on differentiation, the differentiation that distinguishes an inside (of truth) from an outside (of substitution, difference, representation, and the rest). Language as representation must come to rational thought and come to substitute for such thought from outside, as writing is appended to living speech or as a prosthesis is added to a living organism. The opposition inside/outside must already be in place for philosophy to establish truth as what is identical with itself, living, and authentic and to establish repetition, substitution, and the rest as what is not truth (as the outside that defines the inside of truth's identity).

This initial decision to differentiate inside from outside, truth from representation, and identity from difference is never accounted for in western philosophy; it is always simply assumed. As a result, that philosophy declares difference secondary, derivative, and external, when in fact it is necessary to the constitution of philosophy in the first place, in as much as that must begin by assuming identity. If difference were not already at work, allowing an inside to be distinguished from an outside, no philosophical opposition between truth and its others could be established. Yet, according to Derrida, that prior process of differentiation cannot itself be turned into a philosophical category, one that can be identified or grasped by the mind as a clear and knowable presence, an identity from which all difference had been purged.

Derrida also notes that western rationalist philosophy assumes an opposition between the intelligible and the sensible, between ideas and the material world, and between meaning and signification. These oppositions are parallel to and work in conjunction with the oppositions between inside and outside and between truth and its others, and they ultimately derive from the opposition of soul and body, spirit and matter, the ideal and the physical. Truth is always determined as the presence of ideas to the mind, an internal presence that is almost spiritual in nature in that it is supposedly a pure intelligibility uncontaminated by external signs, which pertain to the realm of the body and the physical. In the western tradition, speech (the voice of the mind talking to itself) is consistently identified with this ideal of truth as an intelligible presence in the mind, while writing, which is a substitute body, a repetition rather than an original presence, a sign of a sign (speech) rather than the thing itself in its living presence, is linked to the substitution of signs or representations for such truth.

Derrida argues that these oppositions depend for their existence on what they seek to exclude as merely additional, supplemental, and external. All the traits of signification that placed it outside truth conceived as a pure idea in the mind, traits such as substitution, repetition, mediation, and differentiation, must be at work if such an ideal (of) truth is to be conceived. True ideas are usually thought to be universal and eternal; they must be capable of infinitely repeating themselves. What this means, however, is that they must over and over again take their own place and substitute for earlier versions of themselves. The very qualities of signification that placed it outside truth – that it is a mere substitute or repetition of something more original – are therefore necessary for truth to exist. The supposedly full plenitude of truth known as a living idea in the voice of the mind has breaks, articulations, within it. To be what it is, it must double itself. It must signify itself by repeating itself. As Derrida puts it, there is a supplement at the origin; repetition inhabits presence originally and constitutively; what seems singular and unique is originally doubled.

Derrida's arguments are quite difficult at times. For our purposes, it is enough to say that he argues that meaning and truth are inseparable from signification, that western ideals of identity are founded on a ruse that obscures the way identity is produced by nonidentity and difference, that meaning and truth are effects of the same processes of repetition, substitution, and differentiation that characterize the modes of signification such as writing that are supposedly external to truth, that originality and authenticity, two values linked to truth, do not precede and produce imitation; rather, they too are derived from a process of repetition/ substitution that is the same as the one at work in imitation, that texts that participate in the western tradition's value system will privilege values such as virtue or truthfulness that are founded on violent acts of differentiation, hierarchization, and subordination, that the banished others of truth and meaning, from repetition and difference to substitution and imitation, are banished precisely because they represent a rich multiplicity of semantic possibilities that undermine the paternalist and spiritualist authority of the western ideal of truth, that what counts as true and good is a ruse of domination and an effect of epistemic violence, a violence that can never be taken into account by philosophy if the ruse is to operate successfully.

Other Post-Structuralists like Julia Kristeva find in language a revolutionary tool for undoing the false identities of meaning and subjectivity upon which western humanist and capitalist culture is based. In avant-garde writers like Lautréamont and Joyce, Kristeva finds a kind of writing that evokes semiotic processes that are subversive of subjective identity and of the barriers that keep unconscious desire constrained for capitalist ends. The western concepts of identity, being or ontology, and truth efface, marginalize, and subordinate the processes of linguistic generativity that make them possible. The orders of truth and reason must suppress the productivity of signification in favor of models of homogeneous ontology and cognitive certainty. But the generative power of signification, its ability to create effects unbeholden to the regimes of conceptual truth, always threatens what it makes possible, and one sees this at work especially in avant-garde writing.

Post-Structuralism developed further in the mid-1970s work of Deleuze and Guattari on psychoanalysis and materialism, and it attains full elaboration in the work of Jean Baudrillard, Luce Irigaray, Hélène Cixous, and Jean-François Lyotard in the 1970s and 1980s. Deleuze and Guattari are psychoanalytic materialists who describe the immersion of culture, society, and human psychology in material nature. There is no distinction between the representations of culture and the realities of nature; they intermesh, and culture is simply a momentary arrangement or form of materiality. Matter has two major tendencies, one toward homogeneous organization or stasis, which they refer to as segmentation and territorialization, the other toward disaggregation, deterritorialization, and flight. Deleuze and Guattari advocate an undoing of all the identities and congealed masses that constitute capitalist society and culture in favor of nomadic flows of energy that cannot be pinned down to a system of identity or power.

Cixous and Irigaray apply the lessons of Post-Structuralism to feminism and to the question of gender identity. I will introduce their work at greater length in chapter 6. Briefly, they argue that the oppositions at the foundation of western culture have associated men with truth, reason, and the mastery of matter, while women have been linked to falseness, irrationality, and unbounded matter. Irigaray is concerned with locating an identity for women that might escape these categorical traps, while Cixous is interested in developing modes of writing, what she calls "feminine writing," that transcend the oppositions altogether.

Lyotard's early work focuses on the tension between figural representation, the palpable design of any work of art, and the semantic content it supposedly transports or communicates. Any work on changing the semantic contents privileged in western culture must transform the figures that bear them. In later works, Lyotard will argue that all thought and all meaning is discursive and narrational. When we enter into social debates over the shape of the world, we merely trade stories and offer contending narratives. Any change in turn would merely be the success of one narrative over another. Lyotard calls the current dominant narrative "Post-Modernity," which consists of a rejection of the Grand Narratives that envisioned society as a project for liberating humanity or the working class or the free humanist individual. Now, micronarratives dominate, and society is organized increasingly in terms of cybernetic performativity – how well people and things function to assure the successful operation of a social system in which information is power and in which powerful corporations increasingly dictate what social research shall be about and what shall pass as real. Lyotard examines the pragmatic nature of contemporary knowledge, the way it is constructed as an expanding series of language games or linked phrases that can never achieve a total description of reality or of truth.

For Baudrillard, capitalist political and economic life has given way to a domination defined in semiotic terms. The modern world is one in which the distinction between the artificial and the real, the simulated and the actual, has disappeared. Now, everything is simulation. The modern media especially are so powerful that events, like terrorist acts, are staged for them. The media creates a sense of hyperreality in which the real seems to be on display in an unmediated manner, but in fact, this hyperreality is a simulation. Disneyland is the perfect metaphor for a world in which representations replace the real. Disneyland makes it seem as if the real is elsewhere, outside the fantasy, but this is simply a lure of power that makes us mistake simulations for reality. The old philosophic ideal of a truth that seductively evades interpretation has given way to a flattening out of truth in representation. Everything now consists of signs without referents. We are dominated by a code that assigns identities, regulates knowledge, and defuses desire in so pervasive a manner that even attempts to resist or revolt are absorbed into its operations. The result is that none of the traditional oppositions hold any longer. The good and the bad, the beautiful and the ugly, the left and the right – all become interchangeable, usable as signs which determine people's lives more powerfully than any economic instance or political form.

5.2 A Post-Structuralist Reading of *King Lear*

King Lear depicts a homogeneous society that undergoes a collapse into heterogeneity but then successfully rights itself and expels its heterogeneous elements. This trajectory can be analyzed from several different Post-Structuralist perspectives. Foucault might describe the play as depicting a change-over from traditional forms of social control to more modern disciplinary varieties, a change that requires the depiction of dangers that make the new methods necessary. Deleuze and Guattari might find in it a description of how one territorial stasis is disrupted by lines of flight and movements of deterritorialization that eventually are themselves reterritorialized, giving rise to a new order. Derrida would be interested in the way order and disorder in the play are formulated in terms of the relationship between truth and representation, presence and imitation, speech and writing. Kristeva would heed how the mad scenes display the power of signification to subvert the ideals of truth and order that language supposedly works to maintain. Lyotard would notice how the play works to efface its own figurality in favor of semantic contents or ideals of truth that it would prefer to privilege over the material labor of signification. And Baudrillard might take heed of how the play expels simulation in favor of a real that is itself merely simulational.

The dowry scene depicts the deterritorialization of an old social order, one organized around a paternal instance and predicated upon the identity of family and state. Relations of consanguinity in the feudal world the play depicts are immediately relations of political alliance. The state is held together by family succession, but as such, it also threatens to splinter, to deterritorialize and break apart into individualized lines of flight which subvert the old organizational structure. The move from the singular or unitary to the multiple is dangerous, and the way the play represents the multiple as dangerous, as unleashing energies that drive kings mad and states to dissolution, suggests how much the play will side with the unitary and be about the need to restore a territorialization organized around a single paternal center.

Lear literally deterritorializes by dividing his kingdom into parts assigned to his daughters and their husbands. He seeks to maintain consistency across boundaries and between members by demanding acts of courtly representation, statements of allegiance, that will act as formal constraints (command words or *mots d'ordre*) on the wayward energies and dangerous divisions that the breaking up of a territorial regime potentially releases. But Lear fails to take heed of the power of the unruly energies, the flows of desire, and the violent lines of flight that the old territorialization that was the basis of his rule held in place. His tragedy is to mistake form for nature, gestures of civility for flows of energy. Or rather, he assumes that such flows will continue to follow ordered predictable tracks as soon as the civil forms that channel them in ways that sustain Lear's territorialization have been deprived of the power that made them effective and authoritative. Lear relinquishes the power of his *"mots d'ordre,"* his command words, yet he still expects his words to command.

By relinquishing his power to command, to "tend service," Lear also gives up his power to punish. Foucault argues that punishment changes from being an act of public violence on the part of the king and his representatives, something done to the body of the criminal, to a more subtle process of discipline and self-discipline that is carried out by a wide array of practices and institutions in society, such as schools, that train good citizens. The good citizen no longer needs to have his body punished because his mind has been trained in such a way that he himself enforces the law on himself. Foucault describes this process as occurring much later in France, but in England it was underway already in the seventeenth century. The action of *King Lear* moves from a breakdown of the old order of punishment (exemplified in Lear's banishment of Kent) through a period of lawlessness and strife to a moment of restored order characterized by the emergence of a new disciplinary form predicated upon an ideal of virtue or internally motivated and self-activated good behavior. By the end, Edmund, who has been an agent of subversion and rebellion against the old paternalist organization of power, adopts the new disciplinary form: "Some good I mean to do, / Despite of mine own nature." Despite the fact that he has been physically punished by Edgar, he must, if the play is to be successful in arguing for the new disciplinary order, become himself an agent of its propagation. Evil must extirpate itself; the good must come from within. That it is still implanted from without is, Foucault would argue, the great ruse of the play. The concluding imperative, "Speak what we feel, not what we ought to say," is still an imperative, even if what it binds one to do is voluntarily adopt the new mode of virtuous behavior, which is of course nothing more than a form of self-discipline, the adoption of external standards and imperatives as if they were one's own.

In this way, the energies of subversion brought to bear against an old patriarchal order are harnessed and made to serve the ends of another such order, one that has mildly revised itself to take the challenge to order into account. One of the most striking features of the dowry scene is the disjunction between external form of behavior and internal feeling, between formal subservience and subjective rebellion. By the end of the play, the danger posed by that difference between hidden internal will and public behavior has been subverted. The ideal of virtue assures that will itself shall become an instrument of control, rather than being the engine of rebellion. The rebels, by drawing attention to the dangers of uncontrolled will, of private subjectivities at odds with public power, have aided power and furthered its ends. From now on, power will be certain that subjectivity and will are part of its structure ("The weight of this sad time we must obey; / Speak what we feel . . ."), that dissent itself will merely help assure the legitimacy of power by making it appear as if it is open to contestation.

The emergence of a new mode of discipline coincides with the reterritorialization of the lines of flight that had been so dangerous to the previous state. A new state is established, a new order for assuring the channeling of energies that prove dangerous when left unrestrained. Like all states, this one, despite the apparent modernity of its disciplinary form, must be founded in the imperative mode ("we must obey"), and it will assure the appropriate segmentation of subjectivities: "All friends shall taste / The wages of their virtue, and all foes / The cup of their deservings." The "order of law" that had initially segmented the legitimate Edgar from the illegitimate Edmund is refounded. That this new order also restores certainty of knowledge and the priority of intent or meaning over signification and representation in language ("You lords and noble friends, know our intent . . .") suggests that the disorder depicted in the play might also be described as a crisis of representation, of the traditional order of representation that would have signification be a servant of reason, truth, knowledge, and meaning or intent. The rebellion depicted in the play is also a rebellion in language or signification against a paternalist ideal of truth conceived as an ideal essence that stands outside and above signification, controlling authoritatively its effects and restraining its generative, semantically disseminatory potential.

In the mad scenes especially, what we witness is what Kristeva would call the release of the semiotic flows of language that underlie all the ordered symbolic modes of discourse in which we live. The semiotic is more immediately linked to the body, physical energy, the unconscious, the biological instincts, and libidinal desire, all the undifferentiated, unarticulated flows of matter that are segmented, regimented, and controlled by human symbolization, the forms of discourse which we use to order our world. The pitched battle between the two signifying modes depicted in the play is indicated incipiently in the opening dialogue, which points to the undifferentiated character of matter (Gloucester can't differentiate between the legitimate Edgar and the illegitimate Edmund) and associates it with the mother's body, the only one aside from a dead one ("thy mother's tomb") mentioned in the play. The mother's body, Kristeva would argue, must be placed outside patrocentric culture because the child's initial contact with and immersion in it represents a fluidity at odds with the segmentary boundaries required for the founding of patrocentric society. In such society, the male child especially must be separated from the mother in order to be assigned a masculine identity, one that implies adopting a symbolic mode of discourse that separates signifiers from signified objects, a separation that solidifies the separation from the object mother. The trouble the mother's body poses for patrocentric modes of symbolization is indicated by Kent's "I cannot conceive you," which suggests how undifferentiated matter withstands conceptualization that depends on logical separation and articulation. Indeed, the mother is depicted as at odds with the proper order of social logic, which she inverts: "[S]he grew round-wombed and had indeed, sir, a son for her cradle ere she had a husband for her bed." Against the alogical confusions of the semiotic is posed the "order of law" that segregates the legitimate Edgar from the illegitimate Edmund as well as those forms of civility or symbolic discourse which seal relations of authority and hierarchy and assure order. Even Edmund participates, initially at least, in these forms of civility: "My services to your lordship." By the end, however, he has fallen entirely outside the order of paternal law and lapsed into confused boundary transgressive relations with women who have been characterized as at least figural mothers of the king-father. The restoration of civil order coincides with his violent separation from them. They are literally placed off stage.

From a Derridean deconstructive perspective, *King Lear* enacts a philosophic tragedy as much as a personal one. The crisis of madness in the play is also a crisis of the metaphysical conceptual regime upon which the play's values depend, a regime that privileges identity over difference and truth over representation. The social order of the play depends on an order of truth and representation. The moral ideals of virtue, fidelity, honesty, gratitude, and the like are inseparable from a notion of truth as an internal essence or ideal identity that exists apart from external representation in language. When Cordelia says that she is "so young, my lord, and true," she designates herself as the emblem of the ideal of truth the play defends, an ideal whose pre-linguistic quality she expresses when she refuses to "heave

[her] heart into [her] mouth." Because moral virtue transcends language, moral illegitimacy will be inseparable from representation. To behave badly in the play will be to speak falsely. The restoration of moral and philosophic order will thus be described by Edgar as a triumph of true speech over false: "Speak what we mean, not what we ought to say."

In addition to a certain metaphysical concept of truth, the play argues for a notion of identity as internal essence. Identity gives rise to character differences, but those character differences are presented in the play as secondary manifestations of internal traits. The crisis the play contends with in this regard is the usurpation of a particular social identity by an illegitimate pretender who refuses to accept his difference (and his derogation) within the aristocratic order of rank. The restoration of identity as the source of legitimate social power consists of the reestablishing of a system of differences that distinguish absolutely the authentic from the imitative or artificial.

Derrida would consider the crisis of representation in the play, which allows truth to be denied, falseness taken for truth, and signification to triumph over meaning, to be a crisis of western rationalism or logocentrism. Like logocentrism, the play portrays truth as interior to the mind or logos; it stands outside signification and can do without its external assistance. Signification is an addition to truth, a substitute whose power of imitation, substitution, and repetition represents the danger that signification might do without truth or meaning altogether, take its place and kill it off. In the dowry scene, Cordelia, of whom Lear says "Thy truth then be thy dower," is the emblem of a truth that stands outside signification: "What shall Cordelia speak? Love and be silent. / . . . my love's / More ponderous than my tongue." She and others describe her relation to signification as one of appropriate delay or deferment: ". . . since what I well intend / I'll do't before I speak" and "A tardiness in nature / Which often leaves the history unspoke / That it intends to do." Truth is always described in this way in the logocentric tradition, as an essence outside signification that could exist on its own and that only secondarily and accidentally (after a delay that leaves true presence behind) enters signification, which is characterized as a realm of empty markers devoid of life or of any essential connection to meaning. Whereas truth is living, certain, possessed by the mind or reason, authoritative, and absolutely present, signification consists of mere imita-tion, empty technique, and repetitive substitutes that usurp the place and value of truth, simulating it without being it.

Goneril and Regan are the emblems of such signification. As signification is an excess or addition added onto truth that is supposedly sufficient in itself, Goneril's speech to Lear suggests her love is "more than words can wield the matter." Indeed, twice she uses "beyond" to describe the limitlessness of her affection, and she implies that reason is powerless to restrain the significations of her love: "Beyond what can be valued . . . / A love that makes breath poor and speech unable." If speech is the representational mode most proximate to truth in the mind, a living pneumatic embodiment of truth which is untouched by passage into the empty monuments of writing and signification in general, Goneril's excessive rhetoric, like writing, depletes the breath of speech. Writing is of less value than speech because the breath of truth from the internal voice of consciousness that guarantees the truthfulness of representation diminishes as it assumes external graphic form. The *graphie* of external signification is breathless, a mere mark on the page, the death of reason unless it is bound and constrained to represent speech accurately and only. Goneril and Regan, in their deceitfulness, their use of signs without meaning, represent precisely the danger that such external signification might not perform this duty. If Goneril's address to Lear suggests the emptiness and excess of external representation added onto a supposedly self-sufficient inner speech, Regan's intimates the emptiness of imitation: "In my true heart / I find she names my very deed of love." Like writing, Regan is a signifier of a signifier, someone whose act of signification derives meaning from its reference to another act of signification. She is repetition, the repetition of truth that, like writing which imitates speech or signification which imitates ideas in the mind, depletes and empties truth, killing it off by taking its breath away.

That the play reproduces certain western prejudices regarding truth and representation as well as speech and writing is borne out in subsequent scenes in which letters play an important role in helping to undermine truth and paternal authority. If truth is linked to the power of the father and signification to the danger of the nomadic and wayward son who threatens parricide against father truth, it is important that Edmund's subversion of his father and of his legitimate rival Edgar is carried out through letters that betray truth. Indeed, in discussing the false letter with his father, Edmund indicates the cleavage of ideal meaning or truth and representation that constitutes the danger of writing: "It is his hand, my lord, but I hope his heart is not in the contents." Later, Kent, whose ideal of plain speech, of a signification that would not betray meaning intent or truth, provides Lear with an alternative to rhetorical bombast, is posed against Oswald, who he accuses of bearing "letters against the king," that is, against the father. Oswald is the emblem of a writing that bears no truth, and it is fitting he also be a servant who betrays his mistress. He writes a letter for Goneril to Regan, and Goneril licenses him to "add such reasons of your own / As may

compact it more." Signification serves a purpose, and it need not be loyal
to intent or meaning. Juxtaposed in the following scene is Lear's discussion
with Kent regarding a letter Lear sends via Kent to Gloucester, a letter that
appropriately will signify nothing more than is intended: "Acquaint my
daughter no further with anything you know than comes from her demand
out of the letter."

The treachery of the servant and the treachery of writing intersect most
forcefully in Oswald's handing over to Goneril of Regan's letter to Edmund.
And it is the discovery of Oswald's letters by Edgar that ultimately betrays
the traitors to Albany and allows Edgar to regain the throne. Writing betrays
truth, but it also betrays those who depart from truth. Like Plato's
pharmakon, letters in *Lear* act both ways, as dangers to truth and as cures
or agents of restitution. The deception associated with such letters and with
rhetoric in general also is two-sided. As Edgar's "conceit," his deception of
both Lear and Gloucester, it offers a cure for the madness, the loss of the
power and authority of reason, brought on by Goneril, Regan, and Edmund's
use of signification to deceive. The play thus acknowledges the negative
power of signification, but it seeks to restrain it. Kent represents the ideal
of restrained signification, someone whose plain speech is meant to convey
only what is intended or meant. Truth requires loyal servants who speak
plainly, do not digress or go astray.

At stake in the play is not merely a debate between modes of signification
but rather the idea that there is such a thing as a transcendental signified,
a truth or meaning that stands outside signification in an ideal ideational
realm. In order for the values and oppositional hierarchies of the play (truth
v. falseness, speech v. writing, loyalty v. betrayal, inner virtue v. external
show, etc.) to exist, a prior fundamental distinction must be operative, one
that licenses all the others. That distinction is between spirit and matter. For
this reason, Cordelia, who is truth in the play, is called a spirit by Lear and
remains absent, like truth from the mechanics of external signification,
throughout much of the action of the play that portrays treachery against
the father. That initial hierarchy permits one to distinguish those who are
essentially noble and virtuous from those who are not, those whose signs
express inner states and those whose signs contrive or concoct an external
semblance of such states. The issue is not only a particular relationship
between truth and signification that the play aspires to safeguard, but also
more dangerously and subversively the power of signs to make realities, to
conjure into being things that might not be true in the sense that they would
not exist apart from signification.

Edmund is the arch-contriver in the play, and it is important that he is
the one least convinced of the ideal of the transcendental signified. He scoffs

at his father's belief that the world somehow embodies meaning: "[W]e make guilty of our disasters the sun, the moon, and stars, as if we were villains on necessity . . ." And he meditates on the way signs create realities, separate identities, out of an indifferent matter: "Why bastard? Wherefore base? / When my dimensions are as well compact, / My mind as generous, and my shape as true, / As honest madam's issue? Why brand they us / With base? . . . Fine word, 'legitimate'!" He uses letters and representation to confound identities of good and evil, and in the opening dialogue he is associated with material indifference, the fact that Gloucester cannot tell the difference between him and Edgar except by "order of law." That the indifference of material nature poses a threat to the rational order of Lear's world is indicated by the fact that madness in the play consists of a descent into such material nature. Madness is the taking away of all the differentiating emblems or signs of civilized life. The "marks of sovereignty, reason, and of state" consequently lose their meaning and cease to embody anything.

Without a transcendental signified, which guarantees a differentiation between ideal and material, spirit and matter, truth and sign, inside and outside, all the orders of law that kept things apart ("I'll teach you differences," Kent says to Oswald) in discrete identities and hierarchical oppositions between the virtuous and the nonvirtuous, everything becomes mixed. Children supplant fathers, the nonvirtuous overcome the virtuous, the sign is taken for truth. And signifiers conjure realities instead of expressing or representing them. The right order of truth and signification is overturned. If there is no difference between truth and sign, the real and the signifier of the real, then one might as well have signs as truths, signifiers as realities. The "tragedy" of the play is that this occurs, that this is allowed to occur, and it begins with the abdication of the father, of the transcendental signified from his position of transcendence. Lear says that from now on he will be part with all the other parts rather than being in a position of mastery and command that transcends all parts, restraining their movement and controlling their potential for uncontrolled signification or dissemination.

Edgar restores not only the state but also the proper order of truth and signification as western metaphysics conceives it. If the negative characters use false representation to lure truth away from itself, Edgar uses false representation to restore truth. Fittingly, he is associated with an ideal of the direct expression of meaning in signs: "In wisdom I should ask thy name, / But since thy outside looks so fair and warlike, / And that thy tongue some say of breeding breathes . . ." Edgar, like Cordelia, does not need external signs ("thy name") in order to be truly what he is. The pneumatic metaphor ("breathes") suggests an association with inner speech and therefore with a more true truth than is found in external signification. All his physical signs directly express his internal essence ("breeding"). As Cordelia is linked to the Christian story of incarnation ("O dear Father, / It is thy business that I go about"), which is one model for the western theory that signs embody spiritual meaning and that there is a distinction between ideation and matter, so also Edgar is associated with Christian prophesy, with a mode of signification that immediately embodies truth as presence: "Methought thy very gait did prophesy / A royal nobleness." Here again, Edgar's signs are directly expressive of truth conceived as an inner essence. Edgar's conclusion to the play, which is presented as a prescription for assuring such tragedies do not indeed occur, is as prescriptive as the relation between truth and sign itself: "Speak what we feel, not what we ought to say." Signs, in other words, should embody internal essences rather than be fashioned fit to external constraints, conventions, or necessities. They should be speech, not writing.

A deconstructive critic would argue that this oppositional value system conceals its own constitution in the very thing it subordinates and declares secondary, which is to say, in difference. According to the play's metaphysics, internal essences like virtue are identities that then give rise to differences (between an Edgar and an Edmund, for example, or more tellingly, between a Kent and an Oswald). Cordelia's truth is something silent which she keeps to herself in her own mind, not betraying it in external shows of signification. Such signification is nonidentical and is constructed through differentiations between terms. Goneril and Regan's protestations of love are comparative rather than singular. These essentialist ideals and the oppositions to which they give rise depend on a distinction between the ideal, the essential, and the true on the one hand and the material, the nonessential, and the false on the other. All signifying matter is merely a repetition, a substitution, and an imitation in relation to truth. It is defined by constraining conventions, articulations between parts, and the citation of codes, all of which deprive it of a voice, a purely expressive delivery of truth in its living essence or presence. What is articulated and conventional is a machine, a technique, an external contrivance with spaces between its parts, like the spaces between letters in writing. They oblige a pause, a deferment, and a difference that can never be compatible with the shining or breathing forth of truth in its unarticulated and unmediated purity. Nor is such fashioning fit compatible with virtue conceived as inner nobility, as Edmund demonstrates.

Yet strive as it will to expel the qualities of signification and writing from truth and speech, the play nevertheless suggests that its ideals are essentially and originally contaminated and compromised by what they seek to expel. Spirit never sheds matter, in fact is matter, and truth never sheds signification, in fact is signification. Not that truth enters signification according to some necessity of being incarnated or embodied and is thereby fulfilled. Rather, there never was any truth as the play and metaphysics conceive it as something outside signification; there always only was signification and nothing else.

In this regard, the most important distinction in the play is the one that places convention, the conventions especially that make the marks of writing capable of signifying, outside truth. Goneril and Regan's rhetorical protestations of love are conventional because they cite external codes, imitate models of affectionate statements, repeat previous discourses, and substitute such articulations of models, codes, and discourses for the direct expression, immediate and palpable, of internal truth. Yet when Cordelia speaks to Lear, it is to state her true love as a conventional relationship: "I love your Majesty / According to my bond, no more nor less. / . . .You have begot me, bred me, loved me. I / Return those duties back as are right fit . . ." Her love, in other words, cites a code or a model, albeit a different one from those informing her sisters' speeches. Similarly, when the loyal Kent speaks plainly to Oswald, Regan, and Cornwall and teaches them "differences," which is to say, the need to respect internal identities and essences, the authority that he sees in Lear and that he believes they should also see, he discovers that internal essence is meaningless without the support, originally and constitutively, of external convention. The king should be directly embodied in his representatives or messengers according to the metaphysical theory of truth, but that is only the case if others feel obliged to recognize this convention. When Kent is put in the stocks, Gloucester warns: "The King must take it ill / That he, so slightly valued in his messenger, / Should have him thus restrained." Cornwall's response is "I'll answer that," which means, of course, that he will not answer in accordance with the dictates of the code supposedly at work in Kent's representation of Lear. For the king's truth to go so astray, it must be originally contaminated by the weakness to which it falls prey, must already contain the potential to be unrecognized. And that is because the "Authority" which Kent thinks he sees in Lear's face and which he mistakes for an internal essence or truth is in fact externally supplied by and derived from the convention that allows someone to possess authority, with authority here meaning the power to have one's representations or one's messengers recognized and obeyed. There is no authority without a subsequent confirmation on the level of signification, which is to say, there is no authority as metaphysics (and Kent) conceives it. The author of authority always comes after the fact of authority, as that necessary representation and confirmation without which there would be no authority.

Lear himself discovers this internal fissure and danger – that power, authority, and truth might be conventions, mere repetitions of codes, rather than essences whose expression compels recognition – in his encounters with Goneril and Regan, encounters which provoke him to lose his sense of an internal identity. He does so because his identity comes from without, is supplied by signifiers, "the marks of sovereignty, knowledge, and reason." That his identity is so dependent on marks or on writing suggests that the essences the play seeks to safeguard suffer from an original defect which consists of the need for external supplementation in order to be what they supposedly are in themselves. If at the origin or in the essence of Lear's authority is a mark of sovereignty that comes from outside (which of course makes it a re-mark, an original doubling without which its supposed present identity could not exist), then his origin is secondary in relation to that which signifies it, is given or supplied by what supposedly is added on to it.

The ideal of the direct expression of truth conceived as an internal essence of the mind is realized most forcefully in Lear's performatives, his curses and commands particularly ("Into her womb convey sterility," "The King . . . commands, tends service"). In a converse version of the metaphysical ideal of truth, he uses language to directly bring into being, to make present, the thing he names. He banishes Kent and Cordelia and denounces Goneril. Yet when he reaches Regan and "commands, tends service," he receives no appropriate reply. He himself names the problem when, a few lines later, he accuses Goneril of scanting the "offices of nature" and the "dues of gratitude," images that suggest the complicity of convention and essence, the nonidentical articulation of external models ("offices," "dues") and supposedly internal identities ("nature," "gratitude"). The play would like us to read the difference between Lear and his daughters Goneril and Regan as an opposition between truth and falsity, virtue and vice, nobility and treachery, good and evil, essence and errant signification, but it also points to the possibility that all of these oppositions can be deciphered as versions of the same, so that the ideals of nobility might be understood as treachery towards other possible social ideals, the play's virtue understood as a very parochial, class-based brand of viciousness, its good understood as a species of evil, and so on. Lear mistakes the "additions to a king" (his following of knights, etc.) for supplements to a royal essence, but in fact, as Goneril and Regan rightly point out, the additions are what make the king originally a king. Without an external exercise of force, after all, virtue would not triumph in the play.

Finally, at the end of the play, Edmund is portrayed negatively for having contracted with both Regan and Goneril, while others, Edgar especially, act in accordance with more virtuous inner motives that stand aloof from the play of articulation and signification in such contracting. Whereas Edmund falsely adopts the external mark of nobility by taking the name Gloucester, thereby hoping to use inessential conventions to generate a semblance of an internal reality or truth, Edgar puts aside all the external marks of nobility yet acts more nobly. Of him even Edmund is obliged to say "Th'hast spoken right. 'Tis true." If Edgar restores the priority of truth over signification, he reconnects that truth with authority: "The weight of this sad time we must obey; / Speak what we feel, not what we ought to say." Yet just as he resorts to a different contract from Edmund's, that of the martial code for testing truthfulness and virtue, so also while apparently voicing the play's ideal of an inner truth that stands apart from determination by external conventions or linguistic contracts, from, in other words, writing, he portrays truth as an imperative and as a citation (with all that this implies of imitation, substitution, and repetition, all the qualities of writing that place it outside inner truth and speech). What he essentially says is "we ought to, nay must, say what we feel." The "not what we ought to say" that follows refers to external conventions of the kind that Goneril and Regan obeyed and that the truthful Cordelia did not. Yet the fact that truth ("what we feel") is itself the effect of a prior ought, an imperative that it cites ("we must obey," "[we must] speak what we feel") suggests the complicity of convention and expression, truth and signification, inner essence and external articulation that I have noted already.

In order for feeling to be spoken, signification must be at work, and if signification is at work, so is convention, an "ought" or a set of rules that govern the expression of content in form, of meaning in signification. No doctrine of truth can elude this necessity by claiming to be exempt from its compulsion. For feeling to speak or be spoken, it must enter repetition and substitution, and speech must imitate feeling. That is the rule of representation that the metaphysical ideal of a transcendental signified, of a truth that can stand outside signification and do without it altogether, refuses to acknowledge. And it refuses because the dangers attendant upon writing and external signification in general, the dangers of unpredictable effects, of uncertain knowledge, and of meanings going astray, can never be fully and completely exiled from truth as metaphysical philosophy (and *King Lear*) conceives it.

"I cannot conceive you," Kent says to Gloucester, when Gloucester cannot tell the difference between his two sons. Conception or knowledge requires the differentiation of separate identities, but in order for this to occur, the origin of identity in difference, in an act of differentiation, must be forgotten. Forgotten as well must be the essential indifference of things, the fact that without a concept or a custom of law, Edgar and Edmund would be the same. No identity could be established, no cut made in the continuum of matter that assigns the one virtue and authentic nobility, the other vice and pretense. Differentiation and sameness must be forgotten because they could never be accounted for in a mode of knowledge based on identities. That would already be to turn difference into identity, to begin with one's conclusion. For what differentiation and sameness imply is that prior to knowledge conceived as the establishing of identities is a state of things in which things have no identities. In order to argue for metaphysical oppositions between the clear-cut identities of truth and falsity, noble virtue and ignoble vice, speech and writing, etc., *Lear* must ignore the origin of all of its concepts in acts of differentiation. For what such differentiations consist of is the imposition of a model or a code so that form can be made from what is undifferentiated and formless.

The original and foundational values of the play, therefore, such as truth and virtue, are the effects and the products of a fashioning fit, a forming according to a model or a convention. The terms the play wishes to expel and subordinate as the opposed others of its most valued values – difference, fashioning fit, signification conceived as a maker of realities rather than as a representation of them – come back to haunt it as its most original condition of possibility. The play wishes identity (the internal essence of noble truth in Cordelia and Edgar, for example) to appear to give rise to differences (between them, Goneril, Regan, and Edmund), but the play also demonstrates that these figures could not appear to have identities if a prior act of differentiation were not from the outset at work, shaping their identities and determining them as the products of differences, as the effects of conventions, codes, and external constraints. This mixture, this difference which suggests a lack of difference, this complicity of essence and convention, is what the play demonstrates in Edgar's final speech. Internal truth (what we feel) is as much an ought (we must obey) as convention (what we ought to say). They may be different, but they are not identities that form an opposition. Truth (as metaphysics conceives it) is constrained to speak as if it were outside such imperatives, but that of course is itself an imperative, a form or a convention that must be obeyed.

To use Lyotard's vocabulary, the play ends in an authoritarian fashion by putting an end to the conflict of stories and justifications for action through the violent expulsion of alternative stories and story-tellers. That such explicit physical violence and death must accompany the reestablishment of what the play presents as an authoritative truth suggests that when one story becomes dominant it is not because it embodies truth so much as because it is accompanied by a silencing of other stories. Such silencing occurs because no one story can ever stand apart from and above all others in a position of absolute transcendence or authority. The impossibility of such transcendence is signaled in the play by the very violence that makes it seem possible.

Finally, Baudrillard's description of the emergence of the notion of the counterfeit in the Renaissance would seem confirmed by the play. Evil in the play's world is what is counterfeit, what betrays the true and natural relations in family and society particularly. Yet the impossibility of linking signs to natural grounds, so that signs begin to appear to have a life of their own, also is signaled by the fact that evil as well as good characters emerge from the same nature and the same families. Edmund may suffer from illegitimacy, and share as a result less of a nature with Edgar, but Goneril and Regan are the same nature as Cordelia. The signs of nobility might be attributed to inner virtue, but that cannot be naturally consistent in the way that an ideal of noble lineage would seem to require. Aristocracy cannot depend on an arbitrary allocation of signs of aristocracy, a distribution that has no reason to respect class lines. What one sees emerging in the play is the triumph of pure artifice over nature, of signs over realities. The restored nobility assign to Lear absolute authority, yet the play has depicted just to what degree such authority is not in the least inherent and can only be assigned (or a-signed). The play depicts not a restoration of a natural order, as if signs gave back what they had taken away, but rather the beginning of simulation, the replacement of nature (or of what should have been nature) with a signifying process that fabricates something apparently natural, a relation of political authority that is in fact nothing more than a relation of semiotic authority.

5.3 A Post-Structuralist Reading of Elizabeth Bishop's "Crusoe in England"

Bishop's "Crusoe in England" is a poem about disincarnation. In Cleanth Brooks' reading of Keats' "Ode on a Grecian Urn," the urn is the incarnation of meaning, a particular object that carries within it a universal significance or truth; it points to a spiritual realm beyond human endeavor and outside human time. There, eternal existence is possible. Art objects can signify such a spiritual realm because they possess qualities, such as truth and beauty, that are eternal, that transcend the transient world of decay and death. Like the urn whose truth withstands change, poetry provides brief access to the timeless spiritual realm of eternity. It is a kind of revelation, an opening in the arena of limited, time-bound material existence that allows a spiritual light to shine through.

This incarnational theory of poetry is generally referred to as Romantic. It harks back to writers like Coleridge and Wordsworth who found spiritual meanings in nature. Spirit, they thought, embodies itself in the simplest things, and this lends ordinary life a quality of romance, as if it meant more than it might ordinarily seem to mean. In one of the most famous moments of Romantic poetry, Wordsworth, upon seeing Mont Blanc for the first time, has a vision of spirit revealed in nature. Nature becomes a grand metaphor, a sign that permits low matter to reveal spiritual truth.

Another way of wording the Romantic and New Critical claim regarding the presence of spiritual meaning in nature is to say that everyday life, with all of its petty aggravations, its drudgery, its humdrum routines, its evidence of fallibility, its limitations, its sheer physicality, and the like, is not what matters, nor is it really what it appears to be. What matters is the spiritual meaning that such life embodies. Life is significant for what lies outside life; its importance resides in its being a sign of some other world. This is a fairly grand claim about meaning, not to say about life, and one might say that it describes the meaning of meaning in literary theory. Meaning is spirit embodied in matter, and matter (or language) is embodied meaning.

Considered from a deconstructive perspective, this theory would qualify as an example of logocentrism. Truth (another word for meaning) shines forth through the world of appearances and through literary signs, and it exists outside those appearances and signs. The presence of truth is represented in language and in the world. It is a transcendental signified which guarantees that everything will be significant, that everything will have some meaning implied by it, and that nothing will not be meaningful. Even the blanks on a page that give contour to letters that bear spirit-laden words must somehow mean and are conduits for the general radiation of truth, a truth which infuses even the most technical or mechanical parts of the signifying apparatus that is poetic language. Otherwise, there is no meaning as Romanticism (and logocentrism) conceives of it – as a universal truth that displays itself universally, not just partially, in nature or in the world.

Meaning in this global sense is a way of mastering the world. Nietzsche argues that humans master the world in the same way that they master their own bodies – through will and ideation, by assigning a "God" to it who controls its operations and by infusing it with spiritual meaning that rescues such physical processes as decay and death from meaninglessness. By assigning life a finality or goal – the afterlife, spiritual existence, etc. – such ideals of meaning and truth transform the sheer random repetitiveness of life, that it consists of nothing more than daily additive physical routines extended in time between a wet beginning and a dry end, into hope-filled narratives which provide a sense of orderly progression toward a goal that stands outside or transcends the endless same repetitiveness. In place of endlessness, infinity; in place of the repetition of the same, the unique and singular journey of the human subject toward his telos or goal; in place of the metonymic connectedness of random things and events, a final metaphor that substitutes spirit for matter and meaning for rhetorical figure. Meaning thus masters the random and accidental character of life by making it seem guided by necessity. The events of life that might otherwise have appeared indeterminate, contingent, and semantically elusive come to be bearers of semantic content.

Bishop's "Crusoe in England" is skeptical of Romanticism (and of logocentrism). The poem describes the physical world in all its drab literality instead of as a site of metaphoric meaning. Things that to a Romantic poet would be elevated, sublime, filled with significance, are to Bishop merely occasions for boredom and annoyance. Yet by placing Crusoe on an ocean island, she evokes the Romantic ideal of an exotic place beyond the ordinary routines that block Romantic insight. Her title suggests that the purpose of this strategic placement is to evoke the Romantic, not to fulfill its generic expectations. "Crusoe in England" crosses a figure of exile with a figure of home, and it suggests that the ordinary world will be looked at with the eyes of exile, eyes that find the ordinary strange. In England, Crusoe describes a house as "uninteresting wood," and that reduction characterizes the way he thinks of his island – not as an exotic landscape with spiritual significance as a Romantic visionary might see it but as an ordinary, humdrum collection of animals and objects whose uninteresting meaninglessness provokes despair until companionship arrives: "Just when I thought I couldn't stand it / another minute longer, Friday came." The trope of companionship departs from Romantic conventions in that the Romantic poet is generally alone in his encounters with nature. Indeed, solitude, not company, is thought to be the necessary precondition for illumination.

The poem opens by playing with the difference between the grand and the insignificant, the "island being born" and its appearance "on the horizon like a fly," and between the world as it is and as we know it, between the erupting volcano and the image, the "black fleck," that "rose in the mate's binoculars." Bishop draws attention to the role of human perspective in any knowledge of nature as well as to the way representation mediates all knowledge ("the papers say," "I was reading"). While the birth of the volcano island suggests the rawness of a first event or a pure apprehension of an object, an origin in nature that would be available for direct experience without the cultural impediments that Romanticism sought to surpass in its quest for communion with nature, Bishop immediately places that origin or first event within human representation. In knowing, she seems to suggest, we record, and any direct experience would seem necessarily and immediately to imply a "book-ing," a grasping, and a naming (". . . and rose in the mate's binoculars / and caught on the horizon like a fly. / They named it. . . ."). Whereas the Romantic would conceive of knowledge of nature as vision conceived as the glimpse of illuminated spirit, Bishop equates knowledge both with vision conceived in more scientific and technological terms (binoculars) and with typography (newspapers).

To experience nature in its first impression implies an immediate repetition, a transmutation of presence into representation. The immediate is always already mediated in this way by the modes of knowledge and reportage that we immediately bring to it. Communion with nature is from the outset caught up in mechanics, typography, and writing. Vision depends on focal length, and the original is already duplicated as soon as we grasp it. Crusoe's island for this reason is "un-rediscovered, un-renameable." And for this reason too, no book, no mode of knowledge, as Bishop suggests in the last line of the first stanza, "has ever got it right," a line that underscores the inaccessibility of a direct first impression or experience of nature in its unmediated presence without the supplemental assistance of "papers" or "binoculars," with all the delay and deferment that the repetition inherent in such representation entails. That line also stands as something of a challenge, as if Bishop were now about to set about getting things right herself.

The "Well . . ." that begins the second stanza places the poem in an informal narrative mode that suggests experiential authenticity, a mode of knowledge that would be autobiographic and participatory, not distanced by more objectivist forms of knowing and acts of naming. The volcanoes on her island are not to be known and named but rather personally possessed ("I had fifty two"). The descriptive language is reductive ("miserable, small volcanoes," "a few slithery strides," "volcanoes dead as ash heaps"), as if the situating of knowledge in a perspective in contact with the world – knowledge without binoculars – brings a more literal sense of objects that is quite different from the accounts one might find in books, substitute descriptions in language that can never get "it right." The variability of what "right" might be is suggested by Bishop's meditation on how changes in perspective change the real: "I'd think that if they were the size / I thought volcanoes should be, then I had / become a giant; / and if I had become a giant, / I couldn't bear to think what size the goats and turtles were." Such troubling of the stabilities of knowledge, which metaphorically substitutes names for things, seems to entail a shift to a metonymic way of experiencing or knowing by random contingent associations and connections that allow knowledge to move laterally from object to object: "or the gulls, or the overlapping rollers / – a glittering hexagon of rollers . . ." In such a world of metonymically connected objects and leveled experiences, no transcendence is likely, no conversion of objects into signs of spiritual presence or meaning in nature. Such metaphoric substitution of spirit for matter, light for world, is not possible in a world in which "the sky / was mostly overcast." One can only move laterally along and among the connected things.

In the third stanza, Bishop continues to emphasize the un-Romantic character of the island. It is a "cloud-dump," and things that might have been sublime – lava running out to sea in marbled colors – merely make "a fine display." If there is no depth of spiritual meaning lying behind and under the experiential planes of existence, then all we have and can ever have are surfaces. The one object that merits a near-religious or spiritual adjective ("sacerdotal" water spouts) is characterized as "Beautiful, yes, but not much company."

Bishop's dismissal of the traditional Romantic trope for praising nature – "Beautiful" – leads immediately to a meditation on another Romantic commonplace, the subjective stance of self-pity, of agony over one's distance from the spiritual ideal because one is trapped in the body and in the world. Bishop's ruminations regarding pity are humorously alogical, and they evoke Protestant theology's concern with predestination and original sin: "Do I deserve this? I suppose I must." With spirit subtracted, the world becomes something to be endured, but rather than think of that situation in religious terms as a preordained trial of the soul, something one deserves, Bishop instead crosses a mild travestying of religious commonplaces ("Charity should begin at home" becomes "Pity should begin at home") with a humorous embrace of existential pathos: "What's wrong about self-pity anyway?" Having put aside religious schematics and spiritualist armature, she is left on the verge of existence without a sheltering sky, yet her decision to place her own experience first also places her on familiar terms with the world ("my legs dangling down familiarly / over a crater's edge," "the more / pity I felt, the more I felt at home"). The inversion of cause and effect that makes home a result rather than an origin, an effect of exile rather than an assumed beginning point, underscores the sense that being in the world for Bishop is being without the usual semantic assumptions that Romanticism allows itself, the sense that the world is familiar and homey and meaningful.

The singularity of her encounter with the world is underscored at the beginning of the next stanza where she remarks of the sun rising and setting that "there was one of it and one of me." This is not a Romantic singularity, however, one that might locate a unique meaning in the experience. The repetitiveness of the sun's motions, that it is many and not one, is conjoined with the insertion of the speaker's seeming singularity in all the other singularities that multiply populate the island: "The island had one kind of everything." The sense of smallness that this multiplicity brings is underscored by her choice of example – a single snail that crawls over everything. Flowers are a commonplace of Romantic nature poetry, and they generally are suggestive of higher meaning. When Bishop alludes to flowers in regard to the shells the snail leaves behind – "at a distance, / you'd swear that they were beds of irises" – the contrast seems deliberate. And as she literalizes all Romantic metaphors, so here she literalizes the visionary drunkenness of the Romantic poet as the product of a home-brew made from island berries: "I'd drink / the awful, fizzy, stinging stuff / that went straight to my head / and play my home-made flute / (I think it had the weirdest scale on earth) / and, dizzy, swoop and dance among the goats." Unlike spiritually inebriated Romantic poetics which celebrates transcendent grandeur, Bishop's poetics is home-made, and she clusters it amongst "the smallest of my island industries."

The significance of her choice of Crusoe as a metaphor now begins to become clear. He is someone who had to make things up as he went along, someone whose invention arose in direct encounter with a nature in which the necessities of survival took precedence to transcendental meditation. It is hard, Bishop seems to say, to be Romantic about nature when you are so absolutely inserted into it. Crusoe also is a lesson in the uselessness of much knowledge in the face of a stripped bare world of experience. "Why didn't I know enough of something?" Bishop has him ask.

What is not known enough of particularly at this moment in the poem is Romantic poetry, which Bishop now directly cites for the first time: "'They flash upon that inward eye.'" The line is from Wordsworth, who is most famous for his daffodils, and Bishop recites it to her "iris-beds" of snail shells. The contrast with Wordsworth is meant to be ironic, if not mocking, and in taking her earlier simile for something real (her shells that seem like iris-beds are now simply called iris-beds), she draws attention to the way words beautify a world that might be quite different from the words. The purpose of her citation of Wordsworth, in fact, is to question this subjective power, the ability of an "inward eye" to edify and generate bliss from a world that is miserable, slithery, sooty, and any number of other unedifying things. "The bliss of what?" she asks, questioning memory but also the Romantic undertaking of finding meaning in nature, which, for Wordsworth, was also a memory of something spiritual in ourselves. For Bishop, such meaning has to be looked up in a book because it is not available in nature itself, nor is she capable of remembering it.

Romantic vision is linked to sight and the visualization of nature as embodied spirit, and Bishop now very deliberately shifts senses: "The island smelled of goat and guano." If vision is linked to the idea that there is spirit above matter and that we humans escape our materiality by gaining access to it through poetic insight, then smell would seem to link us more to the world of material bodies and their odors. Indeed, it would remind us that we are not visionaries who transcend nature but material beings who are part of nature: "The goats were white, so were the gulls, / and both too tame, or else they thought / I was a goat, too, or a gull." Bishop turns now to another sense – sound – and rather than describe it, she fittingly gives it in its literal rawness: "Baa, baa, baa . . ." Like the smells which confound the human and the animal and preclude a separation that might generate a blissful human/spiritual meaning in things, sound hurts and gets on one's nerves.

Bishop now cites another Romantic predecessor, Shelley's "Ode to the West Wind," a poem in which leaves play a symbolic role, when she says gulls flying up sound "like a big tree in a strong wind, its leaves," but these are part of the general auditory annoyance, rather than being anything symbolic. Twice more, Bishop evokes the Romantic in this stanza only to question its premises. She says she christened a volcano Mont d'Espoir [Mount Hope] or Mount Despair, a reference to Wordsworth's famous vision of Mont Blanc. The world as she depicts it can either be an occasion for hope or for despair, and Bishop suggests it is neither in any inherent way, but only in so much as we ascribe such meanings to it: "I'd time enough to play with names." Meaning does not emanate from nature itself; indeed, the homonyms "d'Espoir" and "Despair" suggest that human linguistic systems can ascribe quite different meanings to the same thing, a difference that seems to make Bishop wonder what difference it makes. Nature for her is more like the bleating billy-goat whose eyes "expressed nothing, or a little malice." And when Bishop seeks to literally paint nature, the goat, in her human colors "just to see / something a little different," "his mother wouldn't recognize him." The addition of meaning to nature for human purposes merely disturbs nature's own patterns, boring as they might be.

If nature at its most literal consists of annoying sounds and unedifying smells that express nothing, certainly no spiritual meaning, it also consists at its extremes of natural violence and of an endless sameness. Bishop has Crusoe dream of "slitting a baby's throat" in the next stanza "mistaking it / for a baby goat." The randomness of the association ("mistaking it for . . .") between the two killings suggests a leveling of the human and the natural, an erosion of the difference between human death and animal death. The malice in the goat's eyes has now become something more troubling in humans themselves, in their nature as un-Romantic animals. If in unadorned nature, humans come face to face with themselves and their own naturalness (which means, among other things, their own ability to dream of slitting a baby's throat), they also confront the sheer endlessness of nature, "nightmares of other islands / stretching away from mine, infinities / of islands." Condemned to extension in time and space (what nature consists of in the poem), all one can do is "register" flora, fauna, and geography. One can note the shape of space and the living things within it, all on a flat surface of existence, like the ocean on which islands spread out infinitely. There is no transcendence, only an endless dissemination of repetitive experiences, "islands spawning islands, / like frogs' eggs turning into polliwogs / of islands." From a deconstructive perspective, it's interesting that Bishop returns to the metaphor of transcribing and recording ("registering") when she returns to describing human experience. It is not a presence or a plenitude or a revelation; rather, it is an inscription in the mind of the things before the mind, something extended in time and space that does not contain or communicate a spiritual essence. It is simply what it is, a movement without meaning, life as the recording of life.

The advent of Friday in the next stanza constitutes a mock epiphany, a moment of transformation at the verge of despair – "Just when I thought I couldn't stand it / another minute longer." In a Romantic poem, such a moment would have been characterized by a revelation of spiritual meaning in nature to the poet, but for Bishop's Crusoe, it consists of a friend with a pretty body who is nice. The brevity and importance of such everyday charms is underscored by the brusque one-line stanza that follows immediately: "And then one day they came and took us off." If tragedy in a classic Romantic vision of nature consists of a loss of a vision of the spirit in nature, in Crusoe's world in which surface experiences take precedence to deep meanings or revealed essences, tragedy is of a more humdrum variety; it consists of the brevity of experience itself, of experiences especially, such as friendship or companionship, that relieve the boredom of nature. What Crusoe's blood was full of has now "petered out." And the only meaning that is allowed in his world, that of the knife whose meaning was entirely practical and everyday, not transcendental, has "dribbled away."

It is important that Crusoe compares his knife to a crucifix ("it reeked of meaning, like a crucifix") because the crucifixion of Christ is one paradigm in western culture for a concept of meaning as something that transcends the world yet somehow expresses itself through a temporary entry into the signs of the material world. In the story of Christ, spirit supposedly passes out of the realm of spirit, enters matter and is incarnated, and then returns to spirit. Derrida sees this as a version of western philosophy's story of meaning as an ideal essence which departs the realm of meta-empirical transcendence, enters signs and language, and then returns intact to the realm of ideation. But if signifiers are all that exist, and if what we take to be meaning is simply an effect of signification (as a sense of home is the effect of the experience of exile, not something which precedes exile), then meaning acquires much more mundane and human proportions. It is not spirit or trans-empirical ideas; it exists in signs and in what we make of them in our lives. This more pragmatic theory of meaning is what Bishop proposes at the end of her poem. The knife on the shelf had meaning for Crusoe on his island when he had to implore it not to break; but now, "it won't look at me at all." The "living soul" of meaning was something that looked at Crusoe, that was relevant and therefore meaningful to him. And without that look, that relevance, no meaning exists.

For this reason, Crusoe in the final stanza wonders why a museum would want his old things. They may have had meaning for him, but now that meaning no longer is there. This vision of things is very different from the Romantic one that would see the urn as continuing to embody a universal truth long after those for whom the urn had meaning are dead. But that truth precisely is meant to be one that answers the reality of decay and death with a semantic antidote, an ideal of truth as transcendental presence that continues to exist and mean without being touched by worldly processes. Yet, a deconstructionist critic would note, it can only exist as inscribed, as something written. Writing, the originally repetitive inscription of images on the urn, is what permits it to attain the effect of infinite repetition that is the basis of its seeming transcendence, its seeming eternal meaningfulness. It has to continue to exist despite time or over time, and such continuity is only possible as or in writing, as the mere repetition of marks that spirit supposedly transcends. In Bishop's un-Romantic vision, death cannot be so easily transcended; no spirit abides in matter and prevents decay – "my shedding goatskin trousers / (moths have got in the fur)." The parasol that once had such meaning still works but now seems meaningless. "How can anyone want such things?" Crusoe asks because no universal meaning encompasses and retrieves what once was there and no longer is. Meaning is not of that kind for Bishop. Rather it is what has significance for someone, what becomes meaningful for or looks back at oneself. Friday is the figure for the only meaning that could ever be found in nature because he looks back, and without such a look, nature is simply blank, a congeries of sounds and smells and objects. Bishop concludes by noting his death with such exact temporal precision ("seventeen years ago come March") because on the other side of the transcendence that the Romantics sought in nature, the mythical eternity of art, lies temporal existence, the realm of death and decay which has meaning only in as much as it is marked and as we re-mark it.

5.4 Suggestions for a Post-Structuralist Reading of Elizabeth Bishop's "Over 2,000 Illustrations and a Complete Concordance"

The poem is about an illustrated Bible which contains photographs of Middle Eastern scenes. The photographs can either be taken literally as pictures of actual things, or they can be taken figuratively as illustrations of the biblical stories. Bishop begins by taking the illustrations literally rather than figuratively. She describes the actual pictures instead of the biblical stories which they represent, treating them as travel pictures rather than as religious illustrations. What are some of the effects of this strategy? Think about how she shifts the meaning of the illustrations by taking them literally.

In the second part of the poem, she moves from the images to memories of her own travels. You might consider the relationship between the two halves of the poem. What are the connections between Bishop's travel memories and the Bible?

Bishop wants the reader to think about what it means to have actual things before one's eyes or in one's hands; hence, her meditation on the palpable or literal quality of the page she holds. The strategy obviously bears on the question of religious belief, since such belief asks that we read actual things as containing spiritual meaning, as illustrations or metaphors. In thinking about this issue, you might focus on her description of the tomb and of the Nativity. How does she signal her attitude toward the idea of spiritual incarnation through her choice of words at each one of these moments in the poem?

5.5 Suggestions for a Post-Structuralist Reading of *The Bluest Eye*

Post-Structuralism takes issue with the tendency in western culture to think of the world in oppositions. It is interested in the complicity of opposites, the way things held in opposition by western metaphysics can be said to contaminate one another. When Morrison opens the novel by describing "Nuns [who] go by as quiet as lust," she suggests such a crossing of terms, since nuns usually stand in opposition to sexual desire, much as spirit is opposed to the body.

The opposition between spirit and body is crucial to metaphysics and to the metaphysical belief that the clear presence of ideas in the mind – the spirit of truth – precedes and is uncontaminated by representation, imitation, and substitution, all the hallmarks of signification and of writing. One might expect her novel, therefore, to draw attention to the relationship between meaning and signification and to note especially that the former can be the product of the latter.

She would also not be expected to subscribe to the belief that what blacks are constitutes a reality which gives rise to accurate naming in the process of cultural representation. That would be to capitulate to the position that how her people have been named over time constitutes an accurate representation of a reality that stands outside and before signification and is not in any way affected by such signification (especially racist signification). One would expect her, rather, to have an interest in how reality and the meaning of reality is shaped by signification and in how such signification is perspectival, contextually determined, and informed by differences of power.

Consider the novel with these issues in mind. It might be said to demonstrate the political force of deconstruction. Look for things that have more than one meaning, and note how things or people are assigned different meanings in different contexts. Think of "Polly" and Pauline, for example, or of the Breedlove sofa, outdoors as Claudia understands it, and of Pecola as she is seen differently by Claudia, Geraldine, the candy salesman, and Cholly. How does what a person or a thing is change with how it is signified? How does that affect how people think about themselves? You might also consider Morrison's description of how prostitutes have been represented in novels, or the letter Soaphead Church writes to God in which he describes the ways the meanings of various things are rearranged by people (so that cruelty to inferiors becomes authority). What would seem to be the point of all of these meditations on representation? Think of what Morrison says about Cholly Breedlove's life and how it would require a musical score to connect the fragmented pieces.

The Bluest Eye is in many respects a realist novel, one in which one would not expect to find examples of "modernist" stylistic experimentation of the kind that Kristeva privileges as a revolutionary form of writing. Yet Morrison is not entirely committed to the realist paradigm. For one thing, she fragments perspective into different points of view. Consider how else the novel might be said to contain modernist elements. Note her use of typography especially.

Deleuze and Guattari would be interested in the interplay of territorialization and deterritorialization in the novel and in the way space is demarcated for the sake of power. Think of how space is divided up or allocated. How is black space different from white space? Black space allows a mixing or crossing of realms that might be prevented in white domestic sites. Think of Mr Henry and the prostitutes. Enforced deterritorialization can also be a way of maintaining power. How are Pauline and Cholly's lives changed as a result of migration? What is lost through having to move? Think about Cholly's aunt's death and how the funeral is represented.

Unlike *King Lear* which depicts the question of power in society from the perspective of the powerful, *The Bluest Eye* looks at the same question from the perspective of the disempowered. The play promotes what Foucault calls disciplinarity, and one would not expect Morrison to depict power in the same way. You might consider the novel from the point of view of disciplinarity – how it is enforced or disrupted. Think of the Breedloves especially. Morrison says of them that "The master had said, 'You are ugly people.' They had looked about themselves and saw nothing to contradict the statement; saw, in fact, support for it leaning at them from every billboard, every movie, every glance. 'Yes,' they had said. 'You are right.'" Consider how the Breedloves succumb to disciplinarity. And think as well about how the novel might offer alternatives to such submission.

CHAPTER 6

Feminism

6.1 Introduction

Feminism asks why women have played a subordinate role to men in human societies. It is concerned with how women's lives have changed throughout history, and it asks what about women's experience is different from men's, either as a result of an essential ontological or psychological difference or as a result of historical imprinting and social construction. Feminist literary criticism studies literature by women for how it addresses or expresses the particularity of women's lives and experience. And it studies the male-dominated canon in order to understand how men have used culture to further their domination of women.

According to feminist theory, the subordination of women originated in primitive societies in which women served as objects of exchange between father-dominated families that formed alliances through marriage. While such clan relations have been replaced in contemporary capitalist societies by more fluid forms of sexual alliance, the modern industrial world is still by and large patriarchal in character. Men hold almost all positions of political and economic power, and economies work in such a way that women are more likely to be poor and men more likely to be rich. The assumed norm in many societies is for women to be in charge of domestic labor and childrearing while men engage in more public concerns. According to some feminists, such continued male domination is a consequence of male violence against women. Social structure translates a historically continuous threat of physical force. Rape and other forms of violence such as battery are not marginal departures from a norm of consensual gender relations that just happen to be unequally tilted in favor of men. Rather, they are the central, core constituents of the consent to subordination women have learned to give to men in exchange for not being physically violated.

The western cultural tradition has, through its use of binary oppositions, helped assure male rule. Men are associated with reason, objectivity, logic, and the like, while women are linked to the body, matter, emotions, an absence of logic and reason, and the like. In its most misogynist form, androcentric culture equates women with castration and death. Consequently, some feminists argue that women need to constitute a separate realm outside male-dominated culture. In such a gynocentric universe, female values of care, relationality, and boundary-fluidity would become the norms for a feminist social ethic. Other feminists challenge both the idea and the possibility of a separate realm or identity based on women's experience. They argue that such thinking reproduces male philosophy by positing a female essence that ignores the enormous differences between women along the lines of sexual preference, class, and race. And it misreads the way "women" have been fabricated to perform certain tasks (caregiving, for example) as indices of a female essence.

An important feminist rereading of the western philosophic tradition was conducted in France in the 1970s and 1980s in the work especially of Luce Irigaray. Irigaray argues that the subject of knowledge and reason is always defined in the western tradition as masculine. It comes into being through the subordination of the feminine, which is associated with the inchoate, undifferentiated, formless, in(de)finite materiality of the world that must be transcended, objectified, and categorized into proper identities if rational speculation, the power of reason to form concepts and rational representations of the world, is to engage in ideation and describe truth. Only abstraction from matter can constitute the transcendental subject of knowledge as an autonomous identity elevated above the specificities of empirical existence. The concepts and representations of the subject of reason mirror the world, and the material world has meaning only as it provides a reflection of rational ideas. Irigaray uses the word "speculation" in a double sense of mirroring (specularity) and conceptualizing (or rationally speculating) to describe the relation of male reason to female matter. By disconnecting reason from matter and by permitting matter to be taken as a separate object of knowledge that mirrors rational concepts, speculation establishes the self-identity of the masculine subject of knowledge.

Woman represents all that exists outside that subject and its truth. She is material, improper, indeterminate, incapable of conscious mastery, without self-identity, in-different, formless, and multiple. Nevertheless, as matter, she is the mirror, the specular scene upon which reason operates, providing reason with material for its concepts while yet remaining outside rational ideality. Male reason is therefore necessarily predicated on the subordination of the feminine, understood as the principle of connection in and to matter, which Irigaray associates with the mother's reproductive body. Men, she argues, have always appropriated women's reproductive powers for their own (self-)idealizing ends. Women's powers of reproduction have been exchanged between men to assure male alliances. There is a strong link, therefore, between the philosophical elevation of the male mind over the female body, and the social institution of patriarchy, which traditionally abstracts from women's bodies in order to equate them as exchangeable commodities in the status and marriage markets.

Yet in the subordination of women, Irigaray sees the possibility of a certain counter-power. If at the origin of male identity is a constitutive difference from woman and from matter, then male identity must exorcise its own in-different (or nonidentical) origin – the connection to the mother and to matter. But the repressed mother, in the form of the improper and unsignifiable matter of discourse, encompasses male theory (the power to speculate or form concepts) and can never be encompassed by it. Discourse permits rational thought but can never be mastered and subsumed by it – without engaging in discourse. A discursive remainder always eludes the conceptual grasp of male speculative philosophy. All the abstract ideas of the male logos take on their shape and identity through their difference from and contact with the darkness of a matter that remains an unretrievable fringe around them. In its multiplicity and formlessness, female matter constitutes and simultaneously eludes rational man, providing material for rational representation while remaining essentially unrepresentable.

Irigaray proposes strategies for disrupting the power of male discourse such as playing with mimicry or imitation – the role assigned women in speculation – being deliberately excessive in relation to the logic of male theory, developing a tactile style that emphasizes contact over separation, practicing a decentered indeterminacy, refusing oppositional thinking, and celebrating the sexual multiplicity that embodies women's genital duality. If men require property or identity, women should espouse proximity that is nonidentitarian. These strategies seek an exit from the Symbolic Order, which Irigaray sees as constituted by the transfer of women's bodies into abstract exchange values for circulation between men.

French feminism, as it is called, influenced Anglo-American feminist literary criticism by allowing feminist critics to read the male-dominated canon as a symptom rather than a description. Male accounts of women may be indices of male fears regarding a loss of boundaries, an initial dependence on the mother's body, and the like, rather than an accurate account of what women are or have been. The male tradition could thus be turned inside out, examined for what it flees and in fleeing, misrepresents. Feminist critics could also begin now to understand why women were always calumniated by men. And from beneath the ample heaps of contempt and calumny foisted on women by men, they could begin to ferret out signs of feared female potentials and strengths.

Feminist criticism is also concerned with the creation of a counter-canon of women writers excluded from the male-dominated literary canon. It undertakes an examination of the relations between the representation of women in literature and such social and historical issues as sexuality, the family, patriarchy, and law. Historical feminism has devoted a great deal of energy to the foregrounding of such ignored or marginalized women writers as Charlotte Perkins Gilman and Kate Chopin. Elizabeth Bishop has benefited from this expansion of the reach of canonical legitimacy; for many years, she wrote in the shadow of more publicly recognized writers like Robert Lowell and only in recent years has she begun to attract equal critical attention.

It is important to resurrect forgotten or neglected women writers for another reason. In studying the relations between literature and the discourses and institutions of the family, feminist critics have noticed that positive images of female docility and subservience have been advanced by male writers, while strong women are often depicted in the canon as "madwomen in the attic," as castrating threats to men. Women are assigned qualities such as a capacity for care and sympathy that qualify them for little more than domestic labor and that serve as models for broader processes of social pacification. While not all women writers depart from such stereotypes (some embrace them), many like Bishop offer alternative models of identification or emulation for women.

Feminist literary criticism thus seeks to be at once critical and enabling. It takes issue with the way the male-dominated canon has represented women, and it finds in the literary evidence signs of a counter-narrative, an alternative story of women's experience.

6.2   A Feminist Reading of "The Aspern Papers"

"The Aspern Papers" begins on a somewhat problematic note. "It is not supposed easy," the narrator remarks, "for women to rise to the large free view of anything, anything to be done; but they sometimes throw off a bold conception – such as a man wouldn't have risen to – with singular serenity." The statement presents a negative image of women's capacities, one largely shaped by the prevalent sexual division of labor as well as by the denial of access to education and the professions during the nineteenth century when the tale was written. But the stereotype contains a counter-possibility – that women might be more powerful than men. And it is this departure from the supposedly natural distribution of power and capacity between the sexes at work in the nineteenth century that would be significant for a feminist reading of the text. It suggests that women possess resources which must be repressed if the prevailing understanding of the difference between the genders is to be maintained.

This dual attitude – espousing stereotypes regarding women's comparatively lesser capacities while acknowledging that women possess powers that exceed men's – is maintained throughout the tale. It falls to the narrator to enunciate the stereotypes, even as his female adversaries display capacities of insight and maneuver that ultimately sabotage his assumptions, and this disparity defines one of the more resounding ironies of the story. In the first chapter alone, the narrator tells Mrs Prest that Aspern is "not a woman's poet," yet it is she who suggests how to gain access to the Misses Bordereau. Indeed, she is comparable to Vergil in Dante's *Inferno* in that she serves as a guide who helps the poet find his way into the underworld, an image that itself conjoins great power with a more sinister possibility. The Misses Bordereau bear out the parallel; they are compared to the powerful sphinx ("'One would think you expected from it the answer to the riddle of the universe'") and to witches ("'Perhaps the people are afraid of the Misses Bordereau. I dare say they have the reputation of witches'"). While the two spinsters fulfill the nineteenth-century stereotype of women as beings located almost naturally in a private domestic realm separated entirely from the male-dominated public world, they have the reputation of being witches precisely because they are "unvisited, unapproachable." It is as if the seemingly unified image of docile female domesticity concealed a dangerous duality. Behind the mask of angelic retreat is something dangerous to the men who would seem to benefit most from such enforced seclusion and incapacity, and perhaps that explains the seclusion.

The portrait of culturally enforced weakness is countered in other ways by more violent images. The narrator describes Jeffrey Aspern as a lover who had "'served'" women in a "masterful" way; he may even have "'treated [Miss Bordereau] badly.'" The narrator deals "indulgently" with the reputation of his "hero" by acquitting Aspern "of any grossness" in his own writing on the poet: "[I]t appeared to me that no man could have walked straighter in the given circumstances. These had been almost always difficult and dangerous." The difficult, even dangerous circumstances prove to be the work of overly amorous women: "Half the women of his time . . . had flung themselves at his head, and while the fury raged . . . accidents, some of them grave, had not failed to occur. He was not a woman's poet . . . 'Orpheus and the Maenads!' had been of course my foreseen judgement when first I turned over his correspondence. Almost all the Maenads were unreasonable, and many of them unbearable." Orpheus, the poet singer, is a figure in Greek mythology killed by angry women. The danger women pose to male artists seems for the narrator to reside in bodily energies and emotional excesses that can be harmful to men.

That danger might account for the response the narrator fashions to the witches with whom he himself has to do business. If women can destroy men, then one way of contending with the danger is to retreat into a male friendship that excludes women altogether. In such an isomorphic relationship, female danger could not intrude. The narrator's relationship to Aspern assumes such a form. Of his quest he says: "[I]t bridges over the gulf of time and brings our hero near to me." And later, Aspern addresses him directly in a fantasy, offering advice on how to deal with women. The narrator also imagines himself in Aspern's place with women, and indeed, in a perverse, ironic, and belated fashion, he does assume the poet's place in the Bordereau household, to the extent of romancing the younger spinster in a mock and degraded version of the grand Romantic original. In a curious image in chapter 1, he thinks of himself in Aspern's romantic shoes: "[H]e had been kinder and more considerate than in his place – if I could imagine myself in any such box – I should have found the trick of." He is speaking of how Aspern behaved toward the "unbearable" women who flung themselves at him. The sentence contains both elements of the dynamic I am describing – male bonds and the threat of violence. That in this instance, however, the violence comes from men and is directed at women suggests the defensive function of the male relationship. It permits a danger to be countered through the threat of matching harm, and it draws attention to the subliminally violent character of the narrator's quest to commune with Aspern through his papers.

For the narrator, Aspern represents aesthetic idealization as a means of countering a bodily decay associated with the female characters. The aesthetic ideal is elevated above the contingencies of bodily existence, where time and decay erode what was once beautiful. Jeffrey Aspern in consequence seems always young to the narrator; his eyes in his portrait always sparkle. Women, on the other hand, are described in terms that emphasize their more literal bodily defects and their vulnerability to decay. Both Tina and Juliana Bordereau are characterized as possessing bodies that lack something. Tina's face is "not young" and "not fresh." Her fingers are even "not clean." And the narrator emphasizes repeatedly that she is "not bright." Indeed, in his view, she is weak, helpless, and even stupid. Juliana is "too literally resurgent," an affront to the ideal image the narrator bears with him of the "divine Juliana" of the poetry. In her case, the bodily feature most emphasized is age. She is a "terrible . . . relic" who seems like a "ghastly death's head." Her face is "bleached" and "shrivelled." The two women, moreover, "live very badly – almost on nothing," and Tina remarks: "We've no life." Repeatedly, the narrator associates them with death and with dead animals, and more mundanely, he looks down on their shabbiness: "I said to myself that this was a sign Juliana and her niece – disenchanting idea! – were untidy persons with a low Italian standard." Perhaps the most disenchanting idea from his perspective is their excessive concern with money, which he thinks of in direct contrast to Aspern's art: "[I]t had begun to act on my nerves that these women so associated with Aspern should so constantly bring the pecuniary question back . . . It was queer enough to have a question of money with [Aspern's Juliana] at all." Money pertains to a commercial world that appears tainted in comparison to the ideal male realm of art, in much the same way as the human body, with its dirt and its susceptibility to decay.

Women were usually associated with bodily life because the division of labor assigned them domestic as opposed to public and ideational work, but there are also psychological reasons for why their bodies provoke fear and retraction in men. Male ascension to the status of culturally sanctioned "manhood" requires the acquisition of the power to enter women's bodies. If such a psychosexual allegory is at issue in the tale, then it is important that upon meeting the two women, the narrator begins to conceive of the women's world as "impenetrable" and to think about his quest in violent sexual terms that are linked to reflections on his own weaknesses. He speaks of himself as "not having the tradition of personal conquest," and Mrs Prest, summoning the ideal of masculinity as female conquest, accuses him of "whimpering in her salon when [he] ought to have been carrying on the struggle in the field." At the same time he imagines a violent acquisition of Aspern's papers after Juliana's death: "I could pounce on her possessions and ransack her drawers."

The women affirm their dangerous difference from the male narrator by retreating behind closed shutters that deny access to the object of his desire. The fantasy of Aspern, on the other hand, offers a seamless union, an undifferentiated identity, that, in contrast to the women's decayed and unattractive bodily world, exists in the more ideal realm of art: " 'Meanwhile aren't we in Venice together, and what better place is there for the meeting of dear friends? See how . . . the sky and the sea . . . melt together.' . . . I felt even a mystic companionship, a moral fraternity with all those who in the past had been in the service of art."

The contrast between Aspern and the women also assumes the form of national differences. The poet is "essentially American," and "that was originally what [the narrator] had prized him for." If it is regrettable that Aspern "had known Europe at all," the women, bearing a French name, are almost entirely European, and they have lost a sense of national distinction altogether: "You could never have said whence they came from the appearance of either of them; whereever it was they had long ago shed and unlearned all native marks and notes. There was nothing in them one recognised or fitted, and . . . they might have been Norwegians or Spaniards." The women carry associations of a loss of identity, which can be construed both as the loss of self-boundaries that occurs in bodily passion and as a loss of the unworldly purity found in the spiritual realm of art. The poet's American identity supplies the ground for his artistic endeavor; it permits him to be "free and general and not at all afraid." The lack of artistic fear bears a relation to Aspern's "masterful" behavior toward women, those beings like Juliana Bordereau who succumb to "impenitent passion." Aspern "had given her away, as we say nowadays, to posterity." The sense of possessing national boundaries provides a stronger sense of self-identity in relation to women, whose boundaries and national identities in the tale are diffuse and unrecognizable. And by retreating to a fantasy conversation with Aspern and to memories of that era of national and artistic purity ("my imagination frequently went back to that period"), the narrator gains strength for continuing his quest with greater resolution. He vows to "batter the old women with lilies," an image whose sexual resonances are reinforced by an adjacent image of entry: "Their door would have to yield to the pressure when a mound of fragrance should be heaped against it."

The diffusion of identity is often imaged in figures of water, and it is worth noting that Juliana Bordereau's name contains the French word for water – "eau." It also contains the word "border," which suggests the problem of psychosexual boundaries. The boundaries at issue in the tale are the distinction between inside and outside and between men and women. We have noted that the narrator is outside an inside he desires to enter. The parallel sexual and artistic nature of his desire emerges when Tina becomes his means of access to the artistic treasures he seeks. By romancing her, he gains an ally in obtaining the Aspern papers. Water becomes significant in this mock romance when they go in a boat together on the canals of Venice. The sense of floating, the narrator remarks, disposes "the mind to freedom and ease"; for Tina, "the whole thing was an immense liberation," and the narrator feels "sure of her full surrender." If we recall that being free was an important feature of Aspern's original national feeling, the articulation of artistic and sexual endeavors becomes more striking. Mastery of the world of water, which the narrator demonstrates by giving Tina a guided tour of Venice, is equatable with a mastery of women, of the threat to masculine identity that they represent.

Initially, the narrator projects onto the two women the unity he finds in his relationship to Aspern: "They were for both of you," he says of the flowers. "Why should I make a difference?" But he quickly learns that he "ought after all to make a difference," since Juliana threatens the undifferentiated identity, the fraternal, mystic communion, which the narrator experiences with Aspern: "That spirit [of the place] kept me in perpetual company and seemed to look out at me from the revived immortal face – in which all his genius shone – of the great poet who was my prompter. I had invoked him and he had come; he hovered before me half the time; it was as if his bright ghost had returned to earth to assure me he regarded the affair as his own no less than as mine and that we should see it fraternally and fondly to a conclusion." The narrator's fear of Juliana conjoins with anxieties regarding his sexual identity. "It isn't a manly taste to make a bower of one's room," Juliana taunts him. The "border" she threatens to melt into "eau" would seem to be the distinction between men and women, but she also urges him to pursue Tina, as if she demanded confirmation of what the flowers seem to belie. Such confirmation, however, threatens another distinction the narrator wishes to maintain, and that is the difference between Aspern and himself on the one side and the women on the other.

Access to the women implies access to Aspern, at least as he is recorded in his papers. If the women are to be conquered, it is because they stand in the way of a more ideal union that is isomale in character. The narrator idealizes a man, not women, and the difference between the singular identity and the plural nonidentity is important. The danger the women pose to the identity the narrator has with Aspern is that they might destroy the ideal values the narrator attaches to Aspern, from the preservation of a pure and original American past to the seamless and undifferentiated companionship of art. They can burn the treasures Aspern has left behind, wasting the tremendous value they contain. If the narrator has "taught [Juliana] to calculate" and to desire money, that only makes her capable of further sullying Aspern and the art he represents by putting him up for sale. When she offers to sell a portrait of the poet to the narrator, their literal tug-of-war over it embodies the difference between the narrator's conception of art as an ideal and idealizing endeavor that transcends the world and Juliana's more cynical conception of art as worldly, as something which, its emotional usefulness expended, can be sold or destroyed. Perhaps not surprisingly, when the narrator sees Juliana's "faded unsociable room" for the first time, he is struck by a "bareness that suggested no hidden values."

The women also represent a penchant for relations that disturbs the secure boundaries of masculine identity. At one point in his negotiations over the portrait with Juliana, the narrator almost asks her if she has destroyed the papers: "There was a moment when my suspense on this point was so acute that I all but broke out with the question, and what kept it back was but an instinctive recoil . . . from the last violence of self-exposure." What might be at risk here, in addition to the exposure of his ploy, is the opening out of his own identity to intimacies and relations that threaten it with a dissolution of its protective boundaries. Masculine identity might not be differentiated from the fluidity associated with women, a fluidity whose danger is marked in the next sentence: "She was such a subtle old witch that one could never tell where one stood with her." If masculine identity in the tale is constructed isomorphically, through an identification with another, more powerful and capable male who permits one to know where one stands, then Juliana's variability ("[S]he varies terribly," Tina says) represents the danger of never permitting a secure position to be assumed or established.

What the narrator portrays negatively a feminist critic might regard as a positive strength in the female characters. That strength consists of being able to exist in relation to others, to relinquish the security of a stable, isomorphic identity which seeks mirrors of itself and closes off relations that take it outside of its boundaries. It accepts the dangerous contingencies of bodily and emotional life, without having to flee to the safer haven of aesthetic idealism, where a boundary safeguards art from bodily decay and where nothing ever ages or changes. If Juliana wants money, it is to assure Tina of a living after she dies, and if she treasures the papers, it is not for their "literary" value, but because her most valuable emotional experiences are preserved in them. When the narrator compliments the portrait of Aspern, she says: "It's lucky you thought of saying that, because the painter was my father." And she urges the narrator to establish a relationship with Tina. Moreover, Juliana's variability only seems a threat from the point of view of a need for the security of identity. Her capacities might be interpreted more positively if one considers that she too is an artist, an "old actress" who matches the narrator's duplicity with her own performances. She is, as the narrator notes, full of "craft," a word with both positive and negative resonances.

Yet she pays a price for the danger she represents. When the narrator finally gains entry to her chambers, the shock of discovering him provokes her death. The quickness with which she is erased from the narrative – to be replaced by Tina – is significant. The final chapter begins with news of her funeral, and immediately, the narrator enters negotiations with Tina to finish his quest. Like women throughout the history of literature, Juliana has been an instrument for another, "higher" end that pertains to the ideal realm of art and of male companionship. She has been a token of exchange between men. Tina is similarly used: "If she hadn't saved the papers," the narrator asks, "wherein should I be indebted to her?" He acknowledges that he had perhaps "trifled" with her feelings, but it was for the sake of art and Jeffrey Aspern. As they negotiate, debating her offer of marriage as the price for access to the papers, Aspern plays a mediating role.

Initially, the narrator accords Tina a great deal of power, and as possessor of the precious papers, she does indeed possess the power "to settle [his] fate." But he soon discovers that it is she who expects him to settle hers and that he has placed himself in a false position in her regard. "What had I come back to Venice for but to see [the papers], to take them?" he affirms. Although Tina has indeed saved the papers "on purpose to gratify [him]," she has another possibility in mind, one that takes seriously his apparently sincere attentions. She offers the picture as a gift, but it is with the expectation of return. And the appropriate return would be to establish a relationship in which like meets like, generosity meets generosity. "You're very generous," the narrator says. "So are you," Tina responds, and he reflects that "the good creature appeared to have in her mind some rich reference that I didn't in the least seize." Tina is now possessed of the hiddenness that characterized Juliana; she is at once the sphinx whose "esoteric knowledge" escapes the narrator as well as the witch who begins "to frighten [him] a little."

The expectations of the two characters are radically incommensurate, as are their understandings, and this difference of mind underscores a deeper difference and disunity between them. That difference is familiar to us by now, and it resides primarily in the distinction between the ideal world of art and the fallen world of the body. The narrator cannot "marry a ridiculous pathetic provincial old woman," but he can turn to art, a mounted statue that is "incomparable, the finest of all mounted figures," for consolation. In the same scene, he remarks that he could "touch no meat," as if the things of the body had become entirely alien after his encounter with Tina. To the body pertains change while art offers a timeless stability: "[The statue of the *condottiere*] had seen so many [days] go down into the lagoon through the centuries." Tina begins to frighten the narrator when she intimates his transformative emotional effect on her: "'Well, you've made a great difference for me.'" It is not an effect he intended, nor a difference he can easily tolerate. Fittingly, he turns for help to Jeffrey Aspern's youthful picture: "I but privately consulted Jeffrey Aspern's delightful eyes with my own. . . . I had got into a pickle for him." The isomorphism of matching eyes offers an alternative identity to the frightening difference he has provoked in Tina. Like Juliana, she can only think of the picture in worldly, pecuniary terms: "'Couldn't we sell it?'" she asks. "'God forbid! I prefer the picture to the money,'" the narrator responds.

By characterizing his actions as service for Aspern, the narrator suggests a more profound identification with this matching male character. The turn away from Tina is not a choice regarding possible mates; it is a reaction to woman as such as well as to an emotional and bodily life that threatens the structure of male identity, a structure which takes the form of identification with an ideal self-projection. When the narrator says that he "must renounce," he is stating an imperative that defines his very character. All of the terms of description for Tina's actions and reactions during their conversation place the stress on the uncontrollability of her body and of her emotions: "strange spasm," "Then controlling herself she added," "a nervous rush," "I returned not quite so desperately," "She looked at me through pitiful tears," "she burst into a flood of tears," "In a moment she was up at me again with her streaming eyes." In contrast, the most repeated characterization for the narrator's reaction is embarrassment and retreat: "It was embarrassing, and I bent my head over Jeffrey Aspern's portrait."

The embarrassments of the body and of emotional uncontrollability are renounced in favor of male self-idealization. Thinking what a terrible time he'd had "attempting to control [the papers'] fate," the narrator contemplates an artistic image of perfect control, the statue of the "terrible *condottiere* who sits so sturdily astride of his huge bronze horse." Although the statue "couldn't direct [him] what to do," it is as if it offers a model. Aesthetic transformation allows the narrator to overcome his horror of Tina and her proposal, to control his own feelings in order to attain his ends. "It was absurd I should be able to invent nothing," he remarks, drawing attention to the artistic nature of his deceptions. During his final encounter with her, his capacity to invent in a mode reminiscent of Aspern's transformation of the worldly Juliana into the "divine Juliana" of the poetry is foregrounded; Tina seems "angelic," and her look of forgiveness "beautified her." She has been idealized out of her body: "she was younger; she was not a ridiculous old woman." Once his hopes are gone, however, she changes "back to a plain dingy elderly person." And the tale ends with an image of male companionship, the narrator sitting at his desk contemplating the picture of Jeffrey Aspern and thinking about his loss.

His correction – "I mean of the precious papers" – allows woman to be summoned as a possible referent, only to be dismissed. That she must be evoked as being rejected is significant for the model of male identity the tale depicts. That identity is not fully identical with itself; it seems to require a boundary that separates a space of protected male purity untainted by female difference or nonidentity from an outside that is filled with rejected material, from the body to uncontrollable emotions to women.

6.3 Suggestions for a Feminist Reading of *King Lear*

An historical feminist would be interested in how the play relates to patriarchy and to the patriarchal ideal of women. Women at the time the play was composed were told in the numerous advice books that circulated that it was women's role to be "chaste, silent, and obedient." Since the fourteenth century, writers had debated whether or not women were virtuous or evil, the originators through Eve of the Fall of humankind from the Garden of Eden and from divine grace. As late as 1558 in England, just before the death of Queen Mary, John Knox wrote a tract entitled *The First Blast of the Trumpet Against the Monstrous Regiment of Women*, inveighing against female rule ("regiment" here means "government"). Note the "monstrous" in Knox's title, a word applied to the negative female characters in the play. Consider the play in light of these cultural ideals and these cultural debates. How can Goneril, Regan, and Cordelia be understood from a feminist perspective within this historical context?

Luce Irigaray argues that male subjectivity is constituted through the rejection of the maternal and of everything associated with the maternal body, from matter to psychological fluidity to procreativity. Consider these ideas as you pursue a reading of the play. Notice how the language of masculinity and femininity is used to describe Lear's fall from grace.

A feminist might interpret Lear as an abusive patriarch rather than as a hero with a tragic flaw. You might consider how the ending of the play would be interpreted in this light and how the meaning of the word "tragedy" might change as a result. What significance is there to the fact that Cordelia's death seems a necessary feature of Lear's tragic redemption?

6.4 Suggestions for a Feminist Reading of Elizabeth Bishop's "Roosters"

Feminism raises the question of perspective: what difference does it make to look at the world of men and women from a woman's point of view rather than from a man's? Consider how Bishop's perspective in "Roosters" might be said to differ from Shakespeare's in *Lear*. They describe something similar – male martial posturing – very differently. For Shakespeare, such posturing is a positive instrument for restoring the patriarchal state. Bishop depicts it negatively as a grating annoyance. Consider how she describes the roosters' cries and how that description might be characterized as feminist. Note the connection she makes between male posturing and militarism as well as her criticism of "wives."

The poem has three sections. The first describes the roosters; the second concerns the role of the cock in the Christ story; and the third returns to the initial landscape after the roosters have quieted down. The second section suggests that denial need not be the only meaning of the rooster in the Christ story. Consider how the issues raised in that section might be related to feminism. What bearing do they have on the portrait of the roosters in section one?

6.5   Suggestions for a Feminist Reading of
The Bluest Eye

Morrison says at one point that the ideals of romantic love and physical beauty are lies foisted on women. Consider this in relation to Susan Bordo's argument in "'Material Girl'" (in *Literary Theory: An Anthology*) regarding the imposition of white ideals of beauty on black women. Think of Maureen Peel and of Claudia's feelings about her or of how Pauline and Pecola succumb to popular cultural ideals of female beauty.

Many works of literature are feminist not because they criticize the pathologies of patriarchy but because they offer images of women forming supportive communities or relationships that can enable either the struggle to make a post-patriarchal world or the attempt to survive within patriarchy. Consider the novel in this light, focusing especially on the way Claudia and Frieda relate to Pecola. How might the group of prostitutes be understood in this context?

CHAPTER 7

Gender Studies, Queer Theory, Gay/Lesbian Studies

7.1 Introduction

In the late 1960s, closets opened, and gay and lesbian scholars who had up till then remained silent regarding their sexuality or the presence of homosexual themes in literature began to speak. Their work, along with feminism, helped bring into being a new school of gender theory in the 1980s. Gender critics, inspired especially by Foucault's work on the history of sexuality, began to study gender and sexuality as discursive and historical institutions. Gender Theory and Gay/Lesbian Studies were soon joined by a more activist intellectual and political movement – Queer Theory – which linked gay/lesbian scholarship to such public concerns as HIV/AIDS.

Gender and gay/lesbian theorists are concerned with unearthing a hidden tradition of homosexual writing and with examining the gender dynamics of canonical literature. The building of a counter-tradition is made difficult by the fact that, while there have been many gay writers – from Sappho to Tennessee Williams – few of them wrote openly about their lives and experiences. Heterosexual culture was intolerant of gay perspectives either on the streets or in books, and while women might have been put in the attic for being "mad," gays were put in jail for being "perverse." Wilde is the most famous example, but writers like Elizabeth Bishop and Henry James, who remained "in the closet" for much of their lives, were more common.

While much gay/lesbian work is concerned with tradition building, gay critics also interrogate the very notion of sexual identity and question the logic of gender categorization. They question the relation of gender categories to sexuality and physiology. The relation of such categories as masculine and feminine to such supposedly stable bodily and psychological identities as male and female or man and woman is, they contend, contingent and historical. Not only do traits like masculine and feminine circulate quite freely in combination with biological appearances and sexual choices, but also the meaning of each of the terms is highly variable and changes both culturally and historically. Layer in the axes of class and race, and the meanings proliferate further. There is no guarantee consequently that what one is identified as being (either biologically or culturally male or female) will line up in a predictable and necessary way with a particular set of sexual behaviors or psychological dispositions or social practices. The normative alignment of male and female with heterosexual masculinity or femininity in the dominant gender culture must therefore be seen as a political rather than a biological fact.

In a similar vein, these theorists question the opposition between heterosexual and homosexual, interrogating the identity of each and the hierarchical relation (mainstream and margin) between the two. Rather than opposed and exclusive quantities, they are differentially connected moments of a continuum that includes numerous other possible variations. Hetero-sexuality contains a moment of homosexuality, when the child identifies with the parent of the same sex, or when heterosexual men relate to each other while competing over women, and homosexuality comprises both masculin-ity and femininity, supposedly heterosexual qualities, in highly mixed and variable amounts.

Such possible variations are quelled by the dominant, normative dis-courses regarding gender and sexuality, which enforce what they describe. The dominant discourses assume that there are stable identities such as masculine and feminine or man and woman or heterosexual and homosexual that give rise to the discourses that describe them. But such identities are produced by discourse and by cultural representation. The apparent alignment of dominant discourse with seemingly stable identities – as in the long reign of compulsory heterosexuality – is the result of a politically enforced naturalization of a particular contingent style or form of sexuality that comes to be mistaken for an originating ground through constant repetition and rote learning. Normatively heterosexual men are masculine and normatively heterosexual women feminine because the reigning cultural discourses instruct them in behavior appropriate to the dominant gender representations and norms, while stigmatizing nonnormative behavior. Alternative sexual practices to heterosexual genital contact, for example, are in certain places strictly enjoined. The supposed identities of male or female and the norms of reproductive sexuality are thus effects of enforcement procedures that operate through cultural and legal discourse, privileging certain object choices or psychological dispositions while denigrating (and jailing) others. Such gender identities as "woman" are not pre-discursive foundations but rather normalizing injunctions produced by discursive performances.

In a similar fashion, the continuities between a variety of sexual practices across a variety of possible gender formulations (masculine lesbian, masculine heterosexual woman, feminine gay man, feminine heterosexual man, etc.) are erased and subsumed to enforced norms of oppositional identity (either masculine heterosexual or feminine heterosexual, either heterosexual or homosexual). Contiguously connected, differentially related terms are displaced in favor of essential, total identities. They substitute an entire representation – lesbian – for a plurality of connected gender and sexual possibilities that might include lesbian as one moment but that are not fully reducible to such categorical singularity. Lesbian is internally differentiated into a plurality of possibilities (varieties of feminine, varieties of masculine, etc.) and externally differentiated through its connection to or disconnection from a plurality of other possibilities. It is not a singular totality that stands opposed to another singular totality – the normative heterosexual woman, for example, who in any event generally engages in relations that contain homosexual components, as do men with men.

Gender Studies also examines the structures of male heterosexual oppression, both cultural and social, that have contributed to the marginalization and exclusion of homosexuality. Critics have particularly noted the way the more rigorous forms of heterosexual masculinity originate in sexual panic, a fear or anxiety in heterosexual men regarding their sexual identities. The cultural and social violence exercised against homosexuals originates in part from the instability of heterosexual identity, a fear that such identity may be a contingent construct that serves as a defensive bulwark against a potentially overwhelming reality of diverse, ethically neutral sexual choices and identity possibilities that exist simultaneously in the self and in society. Gender Studies has thus given rise to analyses of the repressed "homosocial" strains that motivate the heterosexual tradition's construction of compulsory heterosexuality and normative masculinity.

One of the most interesting and subversive approaches to develop out of gay/lesbian and gender theory – Queer Theory – pushes this point even further. One argument it makes is that homosexuality is not an identity apart from another identity called heterosexuality. Rather, everyone is potentially gay, and it is only the laborious imprinting of heterosexual norms that cuts away those potentials and manufactures heterosexuality as the dominant sexual format. Yet latent and suppressed homosexuality is queered into being in the various kinds of homophilia central to heterosexual culture, from football to film star identification. Sexual transitivity is stilled for the sake of the labor of largescale species reproduction, but in the realms of cultural play, the excess of desire and identification over norm and rule testify to more plural potentials.

7.2   A Gender Reading of *King Lear*

King Lear was written at a time when homosexuality – or "sodomy" – was outlawed, yet it was also a time when James I, the new king of England, was making it increasingly clear to his subjects that he was a practicing homosexual. He lived apart from his wife and child and lavished gifts – including Raleigh's last estate – on his young male lovers. His court was described in one contemporary account as full of "fools and bawds, mimics and catamites" who engaged in "debaucheries" (Lucy Hutchinson's *Memoirs*, as cited by Alan Bray, *Homosexuality in Renaissance England*, London, 1982, p. 55). That "mimics" is a word for actors and "catamites" a contemporary term for homosexuals suggests a possible connection between *Lear* and the court of King James, especially since the play was presented to the king's court on St Stephen's Night, 1606, a festival that might be counted an occasion for "debaucheries."

Bray notes in *Homosexuality in Renaissance England* that the London theater was, like James' court, a locus of the homosexual subculture of early seventeenth-century England. Parents were afraid to see their sons become involved with the institution for fear they might be "corrupted." Given that *Lear* was performed at court and may have been written for that occasion, it is possible that the play inscribes within itself the link between these two subcultural sites – the theater and the court. If this is the case, then those moments in the play that might be interpreted as making sly homosexual allusions – the Fool's remark that one should not trust "a boy's love," for example – or as lending a homoerotic slant to the play's social allegory – Kent's remark to Gloucester that "I cannot conceive you" – take on an additional significance. Indeed, once this perspective is adopted, the play can be seen as suggesting that not just homosociality but also homosexuality is good for the health of nations. Homosexuality is worked into the play both as innuendo and as a fairly explicit, if necessarily oblique, theme.

The play begins on a homosocial note that very quickly veers into an at least jokingly homosexual suggestiveness. "I thought the King had more affected the Duke of Albany than Cornwall," Kent remarks, drawing attention to the relation between male affection and affairs of state. The remark hints at the rashness and indecisiveness in Lear that will result in the destruction of the state; like a woman – as she is coded in Renaissance culture – he will act on the basis more of emotion than reason. The intimation that a man might behave like a woman seems to evoke a further expansion or crossing of gender boundaries and positions when Kent says to Gloucester "I cannot conceive you." He means he doesn't understand him, but Gloucester picks up on the sexual meaning: "Sir, this young fellow's mother could; whereupon she grew round-wombed." The possible reference to homosexuality is as quickly erased as it is evoked, and it is deflected into a heterosexual framework. That maneuver befits a culture dominated by the discourse and rituals of compulsory heterosexuality, which are enacted in the ensuing dowry scene, a culture that in its religion and its law was hostile to such homosexual acts as sodomy. As a result, homosexuality only appears in the play in glimpses whose fleetingness suggests repression as much as expression. One might even say that by evoking it in this opening dialogue, which is played out of view of the more public events that follow, Shakespeare is noting the closeted quality of life in the homosexual subculture to which he, as member of the theater, probably belonged.

But why make a coy homosexual reference at the opening of a tragedy about a father's betrayal by his daughters? The play depicts a crisis in gender identity, specifically a crisis of the institution of compulsory heterosexuality, an institution centered on an ideal of male masculinity which finds an enabling other but also a potentially subversive danger in female femininity. That social institution is depicted as pathological in its most extreme forms, and the play argues in favor of a new masculinity tempered by passage through the dangers of feminization. One cure for the failings of the old masculinity represented by Lear is retraction into homosociality from the troubled heterosexual sphere. In the mad scenes on the heath, a mock theater is created that offers therapy in the form of love between men, a love laced with homosexual allusions. Lear's mad fantasies are explicitly linked to theatrical exhibition, and one conclusion we might draw is that Shakespeare, by depicting a play within a play at a moment charged with homosexual references, is referring to the homosexual subculture of the London theater itself.

The play portrays compulsory heterosexuality as successfully healing itself and reattaining its dominant status and place after a fall into psychological fragmentation. But the play also depicts untempered heterosexuality as a weakness that has harmful effects. It is prone to incest and to the domination of women's lives for the sake of male vanity. "Better thou / Hadst not been born than not t'have pleased me better," Lear says to Cordelia in a line that is not meant to evoke sympathy from the audience. The incestuous character of his demands on his daughters is made evident when Cordelia points out that his desire for expressions of affection trespasses upon the rights of a husband. Later, he accuses his daughters of opposing "the bolt / Against my coming in." Edgar most explicitly articulates the play's critique of heterosexuality when as Tom he speaks of having "served the lust of my mistress' heart," which equates heterosexuality itself with demonic possession by the "foul fiend."

Heterosexuality is dangerous because it contains an instability: while it would seem to assure a man's identity as a masculine male, it leaves the man dependent on women for certification. Rather than be an identity, heterosexuality consists of a relation or an exchange, whereby male masculinity is confirmed by its other, the feminine – submissive and passive – woman. It is what it is not. Cordelia's "Nothing" in response to Lear's demands for tokens of affection exemplifies this dilemma. At the limit where the heterosexual male and the heterosexual female meet, there is always a margin of error where something needed can be lacking, where a required repetition that confirms by recognizing fails to occur. As the Fool reminds Lear several times, without heterosexual confirmation, Lear himself is nothing – "an O without a figure." Which is to say, given the slang meaning of nothing, he is a woman.

If women are the soft spot of the heterosexual regime, its point of proof as well as of vulnerability, it is because the exchange relationship that establishes that system is reversible. Lear's loss of sexual power is metaphorized as his feminization by his masculinized daughters. In a world shaped by compulsory heterosexuality and the cultural postulates of phallic normativity, the feminization of men results in a depletion of power and authority. If one cannot "command service" both as domestic and as sexual labor, one should not rule. In a world organized around aggressive relations between contending sites of power – a fact emphasized in the play through constant references to possible strife between such players as Albany and Cornwall – the need to survive dictates the subordination of weak characteristics and the privileging of strong ones. That these characteristics should be distributed along biological gender lines is not surprising for the historical moment. What is less clear is whether they are also distributed along the lines of gendered object choice. We say this because those left to rule at the end of the play – Kent and Edgar – are men who apparently love men not women.

The dangerous and destructive feminization of men occurs when women assume traditionally masculine powers, when they, as it were, become men. This places men like Lear, who are dependent on confirmation by feminine women of their masculine identity, in jeopardy. Their feminization produces a hysterical reaction that is figured in the play as madness. That Lear cannot ultimately survive the experience and must pass on power to Edgar suggests just how deadly feminization is conceived as being within the early seventeenth-century cultural gender codes.

Within the Renaissance bodily code, Lear's loss of temper and rash actions based on momentary emotions are coded as female. In relinquishing his power to his daughters and thereby masculinizing them, he says that he will follow a "monthly course," a reference to menstruation. By entering the realm of uncontrolled bodily and emotional processes, he abandons the realm of principle, reason, and law – the realm assigned men in the play and in patriarchal culture generally. He breaks his quasi-legal agreement with Burgundy to provide land as dowry for Cordelia, and he subverts the principles of fairness and justice by depriving her of everything for nothing. The price he pays for behaving like a woman is to become a woman.

When his Fool speaks of him as "nothing," he adds a sexual spin to Lear's loss of power: "Thou hast pared thy wit o' both sides and left nothing i' the middle. Here comes one o' the parings." The use of "Nothing" suggests that Lear will be obliged to adopt a "feminine" sexual posture of passivity to penetration, and indeed, Goneril, who assumes masculine phallic proportions as a result of the territory and power Lear attributes to her, makes him bend to her will in a manner that Albany characterizes in symbolically sexual terms: "How far your eyes may pierce I cannot tell." The Fool's preparation of the encounter between father and daughter is more explicitly sexual: "[T]hou mad'st thy daughters thy mothers . . . [T]hou gav'st them the rod and putt'st down thine own breeches." The image of punishment suggests the submissive sexual position and the feminization of the man deprived of power. He can now be had from behind by his phallic daughter.

Earlier, the Fool had compared the division of Lear's kingdom to the breaking of an egg into two ends or crowns: "Why, after I have cut the egg i' th' middle and eat up the meat, the two crowns of the egg. When thou clovest thy crown i' th' middle and gav'st away both parts, thou bor'st thine ass on thy back o'er the dirt." "Ass" refers to servant ("Thy asses are gone about [getting your horses]," the Fool tells Lear at one point), and because servants were known to be used sexually by their masters in Renaissance England, the image, in addition to social inversion, also suggests the adoption of a submissive sexual posture in regard to someone more powerful, someone who would be quite literally on Lear's back. Something similar is implied by Lear's statement "Persuade me rather to be slave and sumpter / To this detested groom." A sumpter is a pack animal, but it also carries the connotation of putting something (or someone) on one's back. That someone, of course, is Goneril, who now possesses the quality of firmness ("marble-hearted fiend") Lear lacks. When he wishes sterility upon her, he more or less completes her sex-change operation, and when she taunts her husband with "milky gentleness," she assumes masculine power in her own household. It is at this point in the play that the Fool's sexual taunts most concern castration and the loss of sexual power on Lear's part: "She . . . / Shall not be a maid long, unless things be cut shorter." "I am ashamed," Lear says, "That thou has power to shake my manhood thus." And he is described as suffering an "eyeless rage."

In contrast, one important feature of the new masculine figure who takes Lear's place as ruler is his detachment from women. Edgar's martial power, his capacity for violence, leaves him immune to feminization. He is not dependent on women for heterosexual confirmation because his aggression enacts a successful separation from the feminine that is best instantiated in the fact that he has no conversations with women throughout the play. His capacity for violence or aggression also distinguishes him from the old king who in one crucial moment is incapable of saying what violence he will wreak on his daughters: "I will have such revenges on you both / That all the world shall – I will do such things – / What they are yet I know not."

Edgar and Kent, the two characters most capable of restorative violence, are also those most associated with homosocial relationships. Kent says he is "not so young . . . to love a woman for singing, nor so old to dote on her for anything." Edgar's repeated warnings against heterosexual attachments during his mad speeches align him with a similar male separatism. One consequence of the instability of compulsory heterosexuality is a parallel structuring of relationships between men and women on one side and men and men on the other. The dangerously feminizing dependence inscribed in heterosexuality provokes a violent response against women, the agents of potential feminization, which enables a safe separation of the male from the female and from femininity. The emotional needs and dependencies that leave a man vulnerable to feelings of feminization within a culture that proscribes "woman's tears" on a man's face and that mandate a more aggressive, emotionally sanitized posture toward the world are transferred into the realm of homosocial, isomale relations.

This ideal of isomale relations is not only homosocial, but also homosexual. Lear, by virtue of a passage through a healing homosexuality, moves from pathological heterosexuality ("I have sworn. I am firm") to an acceptance of his own "infirmity." If emotional dependence is disallowed between men and women under the regime of compulsory heterosexuality because it represents a dangerous feminization, it is permitted in relations between men.

Undercover homosexuality is a parallel social structure to compulsory heterosexuality in early seventeenth-century England, and in the play, a parallel world of explicitly homosocial and implicitly homosexual relations offers a counter to a dangerous heterosexual realm. The danger of being refused "service" by women is compensated by affectionate and trusting isomale relations. If the phallic woman feminizes Lear, deprives him of power, and transforms him into a sexual servant, Lear discovers in Kent someone who subordinates himself to Lear's will. "What wouldst thou?" Lear asks him. "Service," Kent replies. "Service" has throughout the play the dual meaning of obedient labor ("The dear father . . . commands . . . service") and sexual labor ("one that wouldst be a bawd in way of good service," "To thee a woman's services are due"). In isomale relations, the feminized heterosexual male can be repositioned in a dominant masculine posture if he receives "service" from another male.

With Kent, the Fool is a figure of homosocial healing who is also suggestive of homosexuality. Called a "pretty knave" upon entering, he is a male correlate of Cordelia, who is referred to later as Lear's "fool": "And my poor fool is hanged." Both are romanticized figures of affection untainted by expediency. The Fool remains loyal to Lear when it is foolish to do so, even in his own cynical terms. And Cordelia accepts loss for the king's gain, even after he has imposed great losses on her. Both are linked to emblems of retraction from the storms of the world – the Fool with the hovel and Cordelia with the cage. If the Fool provides the same "nursery" to Lear that Cordelia in her absence cannot, he disappears in the play in large part because Cordelia returns to take up once again her role of providing service. She is called fool because in some respects she is the Fool.

What these cross-gender confusions (or continuities) suggest is that the sites of retraction – hovel and cage – are curative because they are outside the exchange system of compulsory heterosexuality. The Fool can be replaced by a woman, and Cordelia (a part acted by a boy) can take the place of the healing men because the play moves us temporarily outside the world of compulsory heterosexuality and into another gender and sexual realm altogether – one that we would characterize as the homosexual underworld of London which has to appear under the sign of madness because it was so outside normalizing acceptability. If Lear is to be cured of the pathological heterosexuality of which he was initially guilty, he must turn to homosexuality and the possibility it affords of adopting a feminine posture of emotional dependence without stigma. We witness that turn in the mad scenes on the heath.

Edgar is the character who is most capable of enacting the new masculinity the play demands after compulsory heterosexuality has been shown to be both deficient and dangerous. Like Kent and the Fool, he is markedly nonheterosexual; he doesn't even talk about women, at least while sane, and while insane, all he talks about is why one should avoid them. Misogyny protects him against possible feminization, and from him, Lear learns not to trust women in the way that he has up till now. He is also placed in a subordinate homosexual position without suffering feminization.

When Lear sheds his clothes and joins Edgar in nakedness (save for Edgar's blanket), the visual display evokes homosexuality, and so as well does Edgar's vocabulary of possession, which at the time was associated with sodomy. Sodomites or homosexuals were often linked to witches, were-people, and evil spells, and Edgar's mad speeches are full of such images: "Flibbertigibbet . . . squinnies the eye and makes the harelip . . . [A]roint thee, witch." Lear immediately develops an affectionate attachment to the "learned Theban" and will not let him go. His characterization of Edgar as an "Athenian" slyly situates their encounter within the homoerotic Greek tradition of master and pupil, and indeed, Lear adopts a student's posture toward the younger man, a posture in keeping with the prevailing image of homosexuality at the time as a relationship between an older man and a younger one or "Ganymede."

Edgar undergoes with Lear the experience of liquefaction that is effeminization. He and Lear are naked in the storm together, and Edgar's "fiend" is associated with water: "Fraretetto . . . tells me Nero is an angler in the lake of darkness. Pray, innocent, and beware the foul fiend." In the source for this passage in Chaucer, Nero is called a fiend and is associated with incest. "Angling" is a term for sexual penetration, and "darkness" is linked to the vagina later in the play: "Beneath [the waist] is all the fiends', / There's hell, there's darkness." What Edgar would thus seem to warn against is the incestuous desire of which Lear has been guilty. The reference to Nero also evokes Nero's other crime – having his mother dissected so that he could see her womb. Edgar does not encourage Lear to violence, but Lear picks up on the reference when he exclaims: "Then let them anatomize Regan." The way out of the water into which women dissolve men when they destroy their masculinity is, it would seem, a violent aggression that desexualizes women.

If Edgar is teacher, he also refers to himself as a "childe" or young knight about to be initiated, since his encounter with Lear prepares him for his assumption of the king's place. That transformation is foreshadowed by the acting he engages in at this moment in the play. That he can adopt a role suggests his malleability and the possibility of a change in social place. Theatricality thus supplies the model for repairing the state, for installing a new person in the role or part of the king. But it also provides the model for an all-male, homosexual group of the sort that ultimately reclaims state power. The small acting troupe on the heath that enacts the trial and imaginary dissection of the offensive daughters plays not only with the emblems and rituals of justice and statecraft but also with those of gender. The scene of "Greek" tutelage between the learned Theban and Lear prepares the substitution of younger ruler for older king, and constitutes an endorsement of homosexuality as a reparative alternative to heterosexuality.

Nevertheless, in the end, Lear must be repositioned in relation to a woman, Cordelia. That the woman is someone with whom he cannot legitimately have sex and that her character forms a continuum with a healing homosocial male companion – the Fool – suggests some of the complexity of homosexual experience at the time, its closeted character, while also embodying the difficult representational strategies Shakespeare was, as a result, obliged to adopt. A play about how good homosexuality is for heterosexuality must necessarily attempt to have it both ways, while having it neither way in the pure form (of sexual identity) mandated by compulsory heterosexuality. For this reason, Cordelia, who finally fulfills Lear's desires (that they die in each other's arms should at least evoke the possibility of the Renaissance coding of death as sex, something which has to occur under the cloak of metaphor), is the Fool in drag, but she is also the heterosexual Cordelia because the reigning cultural imperatives mandate that semen shall make their way to the gilded cage rather than the dirty hovel.

The play's ending is noteworthy for its emotionality. In contrast to their earlier fear of taint by women's tears, the men seem to cry in abundance. Their hearts burst asunder, and their love for each other is manifest. Lear's "I am firm" no longer seems to have a place. The pathological masculinity he initially represents is now replaced by another that seems to incorporate what the play depicts as femininity. If women have been like men in the play, men now become like women. Culturally certified traits seem to shift if not circulate. The play is at its most gender radical when it seems to suggest that those traits are contingent rather than ontological or natural.

It concludes on a note of aristocratic gay romanticism ("Speak what we feel, not what we ought to say") that privileges subjectivity over social convention, the pride of the closet over the mandates of compulsory heterosexuality. It does so, I would argue, because Shakespeare himself no doubt experienced the play's equivocal subject position, which is inwardly gay and outwardly straight. As we know Shakespeare to have probably been gay yet married, we know Edgar to love men, yet he must, like James I, stand up in a public forum at the end and pretend to submit to the rules of compulsory heterosexuality. That no sign of that mandate is evident (Edgar is still not linked to a woman) suggests just how tentatively or grudgingly it is accepted. But it is there nonetheless, inscribed in the anti-sodomy laws and in the religious culture that could not tolerate gay coupling. Only in such enclaves as the theater and the court was a gay subculture possible because only under assumed roles could men act out their love for each other. That James' gay court was known for staging plays like *Lear* says something about the necessary theatricality of gayness at the time, as much as it says something about the gayness of the theater. The tragedy of *Lear* is in part that of pathological heterosexuality, which must in the course of the play learn to reform itself. But it is also that of the homosexual man who must live out the form of compulsory heterosexuality while yet experiencing feelings that must remain silent.

7.3   Suggestions for a Gender Reading of Elizabeth Bishop's "In the Waiting Room"

Elizabeth Bishop was a lesbian, although she rarely alluded to this in her printed poetry. When she did – very obliquely – in "The Shampoo," *The New Yorker*, her usual publishing venue, balked at printing it, and the one poem in which she playfully discusses the topic of gay identity, "Exchanging Hats," remained unpublished. "In the Waiting Room" might be read from a gender perspective as being about a young lesbian girl's awakening to her sexual difference. As the poem begins, she is "in the waiting room" in regard to sexual identity, and the poem tracks the emergence of her first sense of being different, of being "unlike" others. It is important that the waiting room is in a dentist's office and that she is literally waiting while her aunt has an appointment with the doctor. A dentist at the time (1918) would have been male, and dentists, of course, are notorious for inflicting pain on patients. The pain the dentist inflicts on her aunt might be a metaphor for the masochistic position assigned women in patriarchal heterosexuality. They must deny themselves and submit to men. The waiting room might thus be read as a metaphor for a lesbian girl's condition as she confronts a normative heterosexual identity that she might think of as painful and alien. A lesbian girl who has begun to be aware of her difference from the heterosexual paradigm just might think of an aunt who submits to it as a "timid, foolish old woman."

Elizabeth's awakening is clearly not without anxiety, and the way place and placelessness work in the poem are important in this regard. So also are her reactions to the pictures in the *National Geographic*, a magazine that was an early popular form of erotica for young people, since there they could see nakedness enjoined in the rest of the culture. Note how the pictures are emblematic of Elizabeth's awakening identity.

Pay attention as well to how like and unlike work in the poem. What does it mean to feel unlike others? What might it mean for Elizabeth to realize that she is not like other women but that she likes them? Note how the issue of identity gets played out as a distinction between inside and outside and how anxiety is remedied by boundaries and exactness.

7.4 Suggestions for a Gender Reading of *The Bluest Eye*

Gender identities and sexual practices are fluid and multiple. There are many varieties of gender experience, from normative heterosexuality to homosexuality to transvestism to bisexuality, as there are many kinds of sexual practices, from intercourse to fetishism. The novel depicts a number of different identities and practices, but the most positive vocabulary is reserved for adult heterosexual intercourse. Such sexuality is associated with nature (images of grapes and grape juice, for example) and even with religion (the cross formed by their bodies as Cholly and Pauline make love). Elihue's (Soaphead Church's) homosexuality, on the other hand, is characterized as "unnatural." The opposition natural/ unnatural is often used to sanction the dominant heterosexual format and to stigmatize gays and lesbians. Look again at how Elihue's sexuality is described and notice how Morrison characterizes the relationship between Elihue (Soaphead) and Velma.

CHAPTER 8

Historicism

8.1 Introduction

Historicism dominated literary scholarship up until the 1940s and the emergence of the New Criticism, which turned literary study toward textual analysis (known then simply as "criticism"). Historicism either studied the links, explicit as well as covert, between literature and topical events, or it described the way a literary work embodied the "worldview" – the reigning values and understandings – of its age. For historicist scholars like E. P. Kuhl (*Studies in Chaucer and Shakespeare*), the fact that Shakespeare refers to a ship named the *Tyger* in *Othello* provided grounds for an argument that linked the play to conflicts in Elizabeth's court between the faction grouped around the Earl of Essex, one of the queen's paramours, and the faction aligned with Robert Cecil, her powerful advisor. And references to Ptolemy's spheres in his plays justified assertions that they embodied the Elizabethan sense that the shape of the social world resembled that of the natural one as science then pictured it.

Historicist analysis passed out of favor after World War II, as the New Criticism took hold. The major schools of criticism from that point forward were concerned with one version or another of the close textual analysis fostered by the New Critics. By the late 1970s, even Marxists had abandoned their earlier concern with economic and social history in favor of a critique of ideology focused on the politics of form. By the early 1980s, the time was ripe for a revolution against textualism, and it occurred at the University of California at Berkeley, where a group of young scholars – Catherine Gallagher, Stephen Greenblatt, D. A. Miller, and others like Louis Montrose at UC, San Diego – launched a "return to history" in literary scholarship. Largely as a result of Post-Structuralism, history was no longer what it used to be – a background of ideas or a field of empirical facts; the new historicists instead argued for a view of history that emphasized the role of representation and discourse in social life. In their journal *Representations*, they conceived of literature as one among many discourses or systems of representation that exist in dynamic interchange at a particular historical moment. The new historicists were particularly interested in how such collective representational systems work in the reproduction and contestation of social power.

The new historicists were primarily influenced by the analysis of power and the historical studies of Michel Foucault, whose work shifted critical interest away from the macronarratives of politics and economics and toward the micrological discursive practices and knowledge / power regimes that construct different forms of domination. The rationalist discourse of the Enlightenment, for example, conceptualized the world scientifically as an orderly and compartmentalized system of knowable objects, and this discourse was influential in shaping the highly instrumental manner in which those in power behaved toward and in the world.

Stephen Greenblatt lays out some of the theoretical bases of the movement in his books *Shakespearean Negotiations, Renaissance Self-Fashioning*, and *Marvelous Possessions*. Drawing on Foucault, the *Annales* school of social history, the cultural anthropology of Clifford Geertz, and deconstruction, Greenblatt argues for a "cultural poetics" that would study the social and cultural negotiations, transactions, and exchanges that go into the making of a literary work. Abandoning certain critical myths such as the aesthetically autonomous work, the formally complete literary icon, the artistic genius at the origin, and the complete or whole reading, he suggests instead that criticism concern itself with the collective beliefs, social practices, and cultural discourses that shape a particular work. These leave "textual traces" in a work of literature and connect it to the extra-textual representational systems of the culture in which it is embedded.

Greenblatt's approach destabilizes the text and argues for a focus on its margins, the borders where it connects through complicated exchanges with other representations in the culture. Frequently, this method entails seemingly contingent connections with anecdotal evidence that turn out to have a significant bearing on a work. For example, a story from a New World colonist's travel account relates to Shakespeare's *Henry* plays, which further the interests of monarchical power by replicating the representational strategies evident in the travel account. Thomas Harriot's account of the New World colony describes the "recording" of Indian voices, so that the natives might be more easily controlled. In a similar way, the *Henry* plays "record" the potentially dissonant voices of rebellious Scottish and Irish soldiers in a way that allows them to be incorporated more easily into the system of monarchical power the plays promote.

Greenblatt's readings generally are concerned with power and the way it maintains itself through representation. Such terms as "wonder" and "enchantment," for example, describe modes of representation that efface the social practices, interests, and desires that motivate and mobilize power. The Renaissance discourse of wonder, for example, permitted Columbus in his diaries and reports to characterize his extra-legal seizure of Native Americans' land as the acceptance of a divine gift. The discursive regime of wonder, the shared metaphors, practices, mimetic assumptions, and root perceptions of a number of discourses from the literary to the scientific, permitted Europe quite literally to "grasp" – to understand and in understanding to (dis)possess – the New World. Representation is thus productive as well as reflective of power.

While Greenblatt describes the link between systems of representation and capitalism, he differs from traditional Marxists in two respects. He is skeptical of the subversive possibilities of literature, and he conceives of history as a realm of contingency and of microhistories, rather than as a single evolving narrative or as a stable reality that is reflected unproblematically in literature. Of subversion, in his reading of Shakespeare's *Henry* plays, he argues that the texts enact subversive possibilities – Falstaff's revolutionary speeches, for example, or descriptions of the falsity of monarchical display – only ultimately to use these possibilities to reinforce power. The production of doubt – by representing the theatricality of kingship – and its ultimate narrative containment is a positive condition of power. Social power is thus not an external referent of the text; instead, the text is itself a move within social power.

According to the new historicists, the relationship between literature and history is one of circulation, exchange, and negotiation rather than of reference or reflection. There is no single historical discourse of a period; instead, the critic must trace out the multiple and complexly interconnected histories that make up an age. While the connections between historical realms occur through representational exchanges, encodings and refigurings of social energy and cultural imagery that are not reducible to the terms of economic determinism or referential reflection, they can nonetheless be described as the "reproduction and circulation of mimetic capital." A culture in part consists of a stockpile of accumulated stories upon which writers rely and which are crucial to the constitution and negotiation of power within the culture. Mimesis or literary representation is itself a social relation of production in that it is connected to status hierarchies, resistances, and conflicts elsewhere in the culture. If new historicists eschew the idea of an overarching historical scheme, they nevertheless also resist the ideal of a purely local, discontinuous knowledge. Representative anecdotes catch the singularity of historical and social contingency, but they also give access to the systemic workings of power at any one moment of history.

Any practical introductory exercise in new historicist criticism entails historical research. Ideally, one should acquire skill in using archival materials. In "Shakespeare and the Exorcists," one of the better-known new historicist essays, for example, Greenblatt reads *King Lear* against Harsnett's *Popish Impostures*, not the kind of text one is likely to find easily in a college library. And even knowing that one should look for it requires some knowledge of Shakespeare scholarship. To get a sense of how to conduct that kind of research, we recommend Patterson's *Literary Research Guide*. Another less systematic way of going about this kind of work is to latch onto a dimension of a work that interests you – say, the representation of the family, or law, or religion (one of Greenblatt's starting points) in a particular author or work – and pursue readings in the available historical materials dealing with that issue or theme. In taking this approach myself, I found that one eventually begins to notice patterns and connections from book to book that allow one to talk about one's topic in a more informed historicist manner. I began with several well-known works of social history such as Lawrence Stone's *The Crisis of the Aristocracy*, *Social Change and Revolution in England 1540–1640*, and *The Family, Sex, and Marriage in England, 1500–1800*; those led me to other other less well-known historical sources such as Paul Slack's *Poverty and Policy in Tudor and Stuart England* and Catherine Drinker Bowen's *The Lion and the Throne*, which concerns Edward Coke's conflict with James I; and those led to primary sources such as J. H. Jessie's *Memoirs of the Court of England* and the works by King James – *Basilikon Doron*, *Demonologie*, and *The True Lawe of Free Monarchies*. In reading those works, I realized that the new historicist claim was borne out. Shakespeare's play and James' prose works participate in the same discourse of power; indeed, each works to discursively produce and sustain power.

8.2   An Historicist Reading of *King Lear*

I chose as my starting point the relations between the way Lear is depicted and James I, the king who ruled England in 1606, when the play was presented at court. A traditional historicist essay on *Lear* might be entitled simply "Lear and James," since the character of the fictional king and that of the real one so resemble one another. A fitting title for a new historicist essay might be "Shakespeare and the Judges," for reasons I shall explain shortly.

The Scottish James I, the heir to the English throne upon the death of Queen Elizabeth, was not greatly loved by his new English subjects. His attempt to unify England and his native Scotland soon after his ascension to the throne in 1603 was turned back by a recalcitrant Parliament. He was a rash and imperious ruler who was given to delivering intemperate, oath-filled lectures to Parliament when they did not meet his wishes or provide monies to support a court lifestyle that cost twice what it had under Elizabeth. The king also had difficulties with the people he ruled. His right to demand housing and food for himself and his numerous notoriously ill-mannered retainers while making his rounds of the country in pursuit of the hunt, something he preferred to sitting at court in London, provoked complaints. One day, one of his favorite hunting hounds disappeared and returned with a note around his neck begging the king to depart, since he and his followers were eating up the countryside: "[I]t will please his Majestie to go back to London . . . [A]ll our provision is spent already and we are not able to entertain him longer." The complaints began to verge on outright rebellion in November, 1605, when Guy Fawkes and some followers were caught attempting to blow up the king and Parliament.

The parallels with *Lear* scarcely need underscoring. It is a play about rebellion against a king that hinges on a denial of hospitality. Lear assumes that those who owe him "service" will provide food and shelter to his retinue of ill-mannered knights and courtiers, who are given to "pranks," debauchery, and drink. The negative characters in the play refer to them as a "disordered rabble" that makes "servants of their betters." James was well known to dislike the duties of office, and Lear's first act in the play is to divest himself of the "cares of state" in order to go hunting, James' favorite diversion. James valued "plain" speech, and the play privileges such speech in the character of Kent as well as, ultimately, in Lear himself ("I am a very foolish, fond old man / . . . And, to deal plainly"). James himself resembled Kent, who like James swears a great deal and shuns pomp, and like Kent, who cares little what people think of his bad manners, James was blunt rather than politic. His disgruntled behavior during his extravagant welcoming procession in 1603 was so obvious it offended his new subjects.

The shift in the play from an initial language of flattery, circumlocution, and courtly elegance to one of simple plainness by the end can be seen as a figural rendering of the changes James brought about in Elizabethan court culture. He disliked the extravagant dress of the likes of Raleigh and wore clothes till the end of their life, a practice which seems echoed in Lear's own disregard for dress when he is on the heath. Of all the meanings of Lear's gesture of undressing, one is the rejection of the court style, with its emphasis on external appearances as opposed to the inner virtues James favored. James' intemperateness as well as his penchant for oaths also seem echoed in Lear's behavior and in his oath-filled speeches with their references to classical mythology, a characteristic of James' own literary works. James loved "fooleries," and his court was full of jokes and pranks, much like the court of Lear, in which a Fool plays a prominent role. Fond of masques and burlesques, James staged scenes with comic or moral effects of the kind Lear arranges for his daughters' mock trial. The daughters' behavior seems all the more reprehensible given Lear's generosity toward them, and indeed, James himself was caught in a similar dilemma: known for his extreme, indeed reckless generosity, he also had trouble getting those responsible for his upkeep to cover his needs. Finally, James and his Scottish followers were looked upon by many in much the same way as Lear's followers are by Goneril: they sought to govern their "betters."

The link between Lear and James becomes more evident if one compares the play with *Basilikon Doron*, James' advice book to his son, an English-language version of which appeared shortly after he assumed power in 1603, and with his *Demonologie* (also 1603). In many respects, *Basilikon* provides both a thematic and linguistic dictionary for the play. Given the importance of the word "plain" and the value of plainness in the play, it is important that James' book begins with a sonnet that argues that kings should "Reward the just, be stedfast, true, and plaine." James returns to the virtue of plainness on numerous occasions ("be plaine and truthful") and contrasts it with "the filthy vice of Flattery, the pest of all Princes." It is as if he has Lear himself in mind when he counsels his son to "love them best, that are plainnest with you, and disguise not the trueth for all their kinne." Plainness is a necessary virtue of a good monarch, as is control over one's own sexual appetites, something Kent and Edgar demonstrate positively, and Goneril and Regan negatively: "he cannot be thought worthie to rule and command others, that cannot rule and dantone his owne proper affections and unreasonable appetites." James, in terms that echo the sexual advice Edgar delivers to Lear, tells his son to "abstain from fornication," to avoid "the filthy vice of adultery," and warns of women who use "their painted preened fashion, [to] serve for baites to filthie lecherie." As if he were counseling Goneril, who places private interest over national security ("I had rather lose the battle than that sister / Should loosen him and me"), James says the king should subject "his owne private affections and appetites to the weale and standing of his subiectes, ever thinking the common interesse his cheefest particulare." He uses the same terms Shakespeare uses to characterize Cordelia (who "was a queen over her passion") when he promotes

Temperance which "shall as a Queene, command all the affections and passions."

Shakespeare also seems to have James in mind when he has Lear take note of poverty and advocate charity on the part of wealthy nobles: "O, I have ta'en / Too little care of this! Take physic, pomp; / Expose thyself to what wretches feel, / That thou mayst shake the superflux to them / And show the heavens more just." James advises his son to "embrace the quarrel of the poore and distresses, . . . care for the pleasure of none, neither spare ye any paines in your own person, to see their wrongs redressed." Similarly, Shakespeare has Gloucester argue that "distribution should undo excess, / And each man have enough."

Finally, James condemns disobedience of parents in terms ("a thing monstrous," "unnatural") that echo the play: "I had rather not be a Father, and childlesse, then be a Father of wicked children." Lear gives vent to a similar feeling when he says he "would divorce me from thy mother's tomb, / Sepulch'ring an adult'ress." Like Shakespeare, James refers to parental authority and filial loyalty as the "order of nature" and characterizes writing against parents as an "unpardonable crime."

James, in his *Demonologie*, describes the power of devils to "transport from one place to another a solid body" and speaks in the same passage of the possibility of falling "from an high and stay rock." One is reminded, of course, of Edgar and Gloucester at Dover, where Edgar speaks of a "fiend" standing next to Gloucester before his mock fall. The "foul fiend" is an imaginary symptom of Edgar's feigned madness, but he also represents disobedience and the danger of broken contracts: "Take heed o' the foul fiend. Obey thy parents; keep thy word's justice." The first mention of the fiend coincides with Lear's banishment by his daughters. Later in the play, the associations are more ominously demonic. "See thyself, devil," Albany says to Goneril, "Proper deformity shows not in the fiend / So horrid as in woman." In the *Demonologie*, James is particularly critical of women who are prone to become witches and succumb to the "greedy desire" for power or for "worldly riches . . . [T]heir whole practices are either to hurt men and their goods." Shakespeare, in this play at least, would seem to agree.

One might conclude that Shakespeare with Lear ingratiates himself with the new ruler of the land in which he did business. James himself had brought a gift of cloth for the playwright upon his ascension to the throne, and Shakespeare seems to return the favor in this play by painting a portrait of a tragic king whose flattering resemblance to James himself would easily, it seems, have been recognizable to those in the audience at court on St Stephen's Night, 1606. But Shakespeare might also be said to take the king's side in a number of quarrels in which he was engaged and thereby to help further royal power at a time when it was vigorously debated in England. Perhaps the most significant of those disputes concerned the character of monarchical rule itself, whether it should be absolute or limited by law and the Parliament. And it is in regard to this issue that a new historicist concern for discursive negotiations and representational exchanges becomes essential.

In *The True Lawe of Free Monarchies* (1598), James, still king of Scotland at the time, makes a statement that would not sit well in England, the land over which he would become king five years later. Arguing that kings rule at God's behest and therefore are deserving of absolute obedience, he writes: "[T]he King is above the Law . . . And therefore general lawes, made publikly in Parlamente, may uppon knowne respects to the King by his authoritie be mittigated, and suspended upon causes onely knowne to him." To the English, who had fought hard to secure their liberties against monarchical power and who believed in the sanctity of the common law tradition, that well of legal precedents that was binding on all, including the king, such statements were troubling, if not alarming. The future Chief Justice of Common Pleas, Edward Coke, was especially disturbed. In 1607, he would advise Parliament: "There is a maxim. The common law hath admeasured the King's prerogative." James, in Coke's eyes and in those of many other Englishmen, was wrong.

In an encounter famous in legal history for establishing the superiority of law to political power, Coke entered into a direct argument with James concerning Fuller's Case, which concerned the rights of dissident Puritans. James' loyalists, who felt that judges were "delegates" of the king and therefore that the king was the ultimate judge in all matters, wanted to force the Puritans to testify under an inquisitorial oath that deprived them of their common law rights. As Chief Justice of the Common Pleas Court that fought for jurisdiction with the loyalists' Ecclesiastical High Commission regarding the judgment of lay matters, Coke disagreed, and the issue came before James. When the loyalists claimed that the ultimate decision lay with the king, Coke replied: "The King cannot take any cause out of any of his courts and give judgment upon it himself." James accused Coke of speaking foolishly and said he reserved the power to decide jurisdictional issues, adding that he "would ever protect the common law." Coke responded: "The common law protecteth the King." At this point, James accused him of treason. "The King protecteth the law, and not the law the King," he declared. To which Coke replied "The King should not be under man, but under God and the Laws." He nevertheless flung himself at the king's feet and seemed to submit. But the next week he commenced once again to issue rulings at odds with the Commission.

I recount this anecdote to give a sense of what the discursive ambience was at the time *Lear* was written. The topics of monarchical power and judicial authority were publicly discussed and debated. The limits of monarchical power were at stake, and the conflict between king and Parliament would eventually lead to civil war and the overthrow of the monarchy in mid–century. In 1605, the year *Lear* was probably written, things had not yet come to that point, but Guy Fawkes and his followers took the debate over prerogative to another level in the Gunpowder Plot in November of that year. Rebellion was not only in the air; it was also underground.

James' *True Lawe* is an argument against such rebellion. Its principle rhetorical strategy consists of *warning*. James begins by warning his audience of just how abusive monarchical rule can be. The monarch will, James warns, quoting the Book of Samuel, take your sons and make them servants, take your daughters and make them "Cookes and Bakers," take your fields and give them to his servants, "take the tenth of your seede . . . and give it to his Eunuches," and "all that ye possess shall serve his private use and inordinate appetite." He concludes "and ye shall be his servants." If one weren't aware that one was reading a work by a reigning monarch, one might at this point think that the author was Guy Fawkes himself trying to raise a following. The warning is subversive of the very power it ostensibly legitimates. It suggests that kings do abuse their power, and it quite accurately and vividly describes those abuses.

Yet the warning also serves to further power. By quoting scripture, James places the question of monarchical rule within the frame of the paradoxical parables of the Bible, parables whose very incomprehensibility serves to reinforce God's ultimate authority, his transcendence of mere worldly logic. "Yet it shall not be lawful to you to cast it off," James argues of monarchy, because absolute rule is "the ordinance of GOD" and "your selves have chosen him unto you, thereby renouncing for ever all privileges, by your willing consent," especially that one which would allow people to "call backe unto your selves againe that power" given to the king. In other words, despite all the great abuses of monarchical power that have just been so vividly depicted, you will have to put up with it. As in biblical parables in general, which argue that one has to learn to accept rough treatment at the hands of God, since it is for one's own good, one must, according to James, also put up with abusive kings, because the king is a step down from God. Hence, he has the loyal people say to Samuel: "Al your speeches and hard conditions shal not skarre us, but we wil take the good and evill of it upon us, and we will be content to bear whatsoever burthen it shall please our King to lay upon us." If the king is bad, God will judge him – but no one else shall. He has the "power to judge [his people] but to be judged only by God."

The king, for James, is like a father in a family. If the people must fear the king "as their judge," they must love him "as their father." To displace the king through rebellion is to invert "the order of all law and reason," so that "the commanded may be made to command their commander, the judged to judge their Judge, and they that are governed to governe their time about their lord & governer." Obedience is the "duty his children owe to" a father, and hence also to a king. It would be "monstrous and unnatural to his sons to rise up against" either father or king. Fittingly, rebels who claim a higher allegiance to the commonwealth, "as to a Mother," are condemned. James concludes the text by denouncing what he twice, using language echoed in *Lear*, refers to as "monstrous and unnatural rebellions" against an absolute monarch. It is wrong for one party to break a contract "except that first a lawful trial and cognition be had by the ordinary judge of the breakers thereof."

What *Lear* depicts is in many ways what James describes and denounces – a "monstrous" and "unnatural" rebellion against both paternal and monarchical power. The play literalizes James' metaphors. Lear is both father and king; the rebels are his daughters. They invert the right order of government when they "command the commander" and refuse him "the duty his children owe to him." They enter into a contract – land in exchange for love and hospitality – and break it unilaterally. Regan's language of rebellion recalls the legal language of arguments in favor of Parliamentary prerogative: "In my rights, / By me invested, he compeers the best."

It is as if Shakespeare had James' concluding argument in mind when he has Lear summon his daughters forth for an imaginary trial, which enacts the lawful reinstatement of the appropriate judge so that "cognition" can be taken of "the breakers." If Shakespeare would seem to take James' part in his argument with Parliamentary dissenters, he also seems, especially in the trial scene, to take his side in his debate with the common law judges, especially Coke. "You are o' the commission; / Sit you too," Lear tells Kent. This is not the first reference in the text to the Ecclesiastical Commission that supported James' claim to absolute authority over the common law judges. Already in Act 3, scene 2, Lear speaks favorably of "These dreadful summoners grace," a reference to the police or summoners who served warrants for the Ecclesiastical Commission or court. Given James' antipathy for the common law judges, it is probably of some significance that the trial scene concludes with Lear's cry "Corruption in the place! / False justicer!"

But what are we to make of Lear's vision of a judge and a thief as interchangeable and his provocative suggestion that judges favor the wealthy over the poor? It is one of the most subversive statements in the play. Yet like the mock trial scene, it is framed by an implicit pledge of allegiance to

James' absolutist position regarding the superiority of monarchical power to the common law. Coke was one judge who had become quite wealthy while in office, and justices of the peace, upholders of the common law, were great obstructors of the poor relief James advocated. The 1590s were a time of harvest failures and of famine. As a result of the enclosure of common land for the sake of more profitable pasturing, more and more farm laborers turned to vagrancy, giving rise to laws regarding poor relief and charity. James was a promoter of charity, and the Statute of 1604 was meant to provide such relief on a more uniform basis. Its implementation was overseen by his Privy Council, but it met with a resistant negligence on the part of justices of the peace, who were in charge of tax collecting and the enforcement of statutes on the local level, even when prodded "by extraordinary directions derived from the prerogative power of his Majesty by proclamations, letters, and commissions." Perhaps this is why one of the most sympathetic characters in the play, Edgar as Tom, mentions charity twice in his entry speech: "Do poor Tom some charity . . . The country gives me proof and precedent / Of Bedlam beggars who with roaring voices / . . . Enforce their charity."

Other seemingly subversive statements by Lear can be interpreted in a similar manner. When he speaks of "the great image of authority; / A dog's obeyed in office," he refers not to the king, whose position as a divinely ordained ruler was above "office," but rather to the holders of political office – the Parliamentarians – who circumvented the king's wishes. The lustful beadle who hypocritically punishes the whore in the next lines describes a similar enemy of the Catholic king whose court was renowned for loose sexual morals – the Puritan clergy. And the "Robes and furred gowns" that "hide all" vices in the following lines refer to the Elizabethan courtiers, like Raleigh, whom James loathed.

If Shakespeare is critical of judges and of justices in a way that echoes James' absolutist positions, the one positive reference to justices in the play also serves the interests of absolute monarchical power. Of the quick death of Cornwall after Gloucester's blinding, Albany says: "This shows you are above, / You justicers, that these our nether crimes / So speedily can venge!" Heavenly not earthly judges are the guardians of justice in the play. The rebels are also subject to "the judgement of the heavens, that makes us tremble." "The gods are just," Edgar remarks, after having vanquished Edmund and set right the kingdom. He is presented as an instrument of divine justice, while also evincing a natural royalty. The force of someone endowed with royal power ("thy very gait did prophesy / A royal nobleness") is needed because legal measures are subject to the contingencies of broken agreements and the failure of judges. "[T]he laws are mine, not thine," Goneril claims defiantly, "Who can arraign me for 't?" A divine judge, James might respond, and in his place, a king or would-be king like Edgar.

The seemingly subversive critique of justice and of judges in the play is a maneuver within a discourse that seeks to legitimate absolute monarchical rule by warning of its abuses in order better to plead for its divinely ordained necessity. "[W]e will resign to him, / . . . our absolute power," Albany says of Lear at the end. Rather than directly advocate such power, however, the play enacts a subversive vision of inversion and disorder whose ultimate purpose is to reinforce that which is overturned and to further power. Initially, monarchical rule is presented negatively. The play begins with a warning regarding the abuses to which kings are prone. Lear rules in an abusive manner. In a single scene, he banishes his favorite courtier and deprives his favorite daughter of her dowry. He is intolerant of dissent and commands absolute obedience. His behavior seems "rash," but it is also typical of how kings should be allowed to behave, according to James, and still command obedience. Kent's and Cordelia's remarkable fidelity in the face of the king's abusive exercise of monarchical power are the positive examples that complete what one might call the warning plot of the play. Kings may be rash, it argues, but we must, like Kent and Cordelia, obey them absolutely nonetheless. Even the infirmity and fury of a king, like that of a father, must, according to James, be "borne." Even as a madman, Lear is told "You are a royal one, and we obey you."

8.3 Suggestions for an Historicist Reading of "The Aspern Papers"

The narrator of the tale is an aesthete, and aestheticism was an important cultural movement in England at the time the tale was written (in the 1880s). But the narrator, oddly enough perhaps, is also a tourist, a relatively new cultural invention. One point of departure for an historicist reading might therefore be James' use of these two cultural markers in the tale.

The desire to see picturesque places, especially landscapes, animated the Romantic movement in art and literature from the late eighteenth through the early nineteenth centuries in western Europe. Jeffrey Aspern has elements of Romanticism about him, and the prototype for Juliana Bordereau – Jane Claremont – was the lover of one of the great English Romantic poets, George, Lord Byron. As Byron's aristocratic title suggests, travel on behalf of the picturesque began as the private pastime of the English upper classes in the eighteenth century, who traveled to distant places like

Scotland in search of the right vista. In 1848, however, Thomas Cook, who had up till then devoted himself to the cause of temperance amongst the urban laboring classes, took note of a new invention – the railroad – and decided to adopt a different approach to the task of moral reform. Rather than uplift the laboring masses, he would instead send them on vacation – or on excursion, as he called it. Cook established the world's first travel agency and began organizing weekend trips to such places as Bath, which were quickly overrun by crowds seeking accommodations that did not exist. Modern tourism was born.

By the early 1860s, Cook, taking full advantage of the prosperity as well as the power of the British Empire, then at its peak, was busy wardening groups of middle-class professionals and their families through Europe, Africa, and the Middle East in search of picturesque landscapes and cities. What had been a matter of private appreciation by the wealthy few became a very public matter indeed, one characterized by crowds embarking and disembarking on boats and trains in search of their own version of the picturesque, one often now capturable in newly invented photographs. Those who had been used to having the picturesque to themselves were understandably upset. "The fortunate generation is passing away," Leslie Stephen wrote at the time. "The charm is perishing. Huge caravanseries replace the hospitable inn; railways creep to the foot of Monte Rosa . . . The tourist dispatches Switzerland as rapidly and thoughtlessly as he does Olympia; and the very name of the Alps, so musical in the ears of those who enjoyed their mysterious charm, suggests little more than the hurry and jostling of an average sight-seeing trip."

A tourist publishing industry came into being, ready to supply the new travelers with guidebooks filled with advice and descriptions of their favorite destinations. Many writers, including Henry James, made an income supplying magazines back home with accounts of their travels to such places as Italy. These books served in part as training manuals in how to find and see the picturesque. In his *Transatlantic Sketches* (1875), for example, James writes of his arrival in Siena: "As I suddenly stepped into this Piazza from under a dark archway, it seemed a vivid enough revelation of the picturesque." And what the picturesque consisted of in part was a sense of the artistry of the world viewed: "There is to an American something richly artificial and scenic . . . in the way these colossal dwellings are packed together." The Jamesian tourist is guided by a sense that the world is art, something to be appreciated in the same manner as a picture in a museum.

But such tourism had its limits. If earlier tourists felt that their private contemplation of places like the Alps was disturbed by the hordes of middle-class barbarians, another kind of privacy limited the scope of the art of travel, and that was the privacy of the inhabitants of the picturesque. James writes again of Siena: "My friend's account of domiciliary medievalism made me wish that your really appreciative tourist was not reduced to simply staring at black stones and peeping up stately staircases." He goes on to wish he might mount the stairs, "Murray in hand," and get favored by the local aristocrats with "a little sketch of their social philosophy or a few first rate family anecdotes." The trouble with so public a venture as tourism was that it precluded intimate engagement with the goal of one's quest. Between the role of tourist and that of inhabitant, there was a small but significant difference.

How might these historical developments aid an historicist reading of "The Aspern Papers"? Consider how the tale alludes to the new tourist industry and what role it plays in the portrayal of the narrator. It would seem a significant choice on James' part that the narrator goes touring after he has essentially killed Juliana. How else is tourism portrayed in the tale?

The aesthetic movement came into being in the mid-nineteenth century at the same time as mass tourism. It emphasized either the otherworldly and moral or the subjective and private qualities of art and of artistic experience. The two great works of the aesthetic movement were John Ruskin's *The Stones of Venice* (1849) and Walter Pater's *The Renaissance* (1873). The first argued for a moral vision of architecture, while the second celebrated the sensuous experience of art. James was aware of both books. "It is Mr. Ruskin," he writes in his *Portraits of Places*, "who, beyond any one, helps us to enjoy [Venice]." The trouble was that he also helped crowds of others to enjoy as well. In celebrating Venice, Ruskin advertised it to the masses and helped make it a favorite stopping-place for tourists.

Paterian aestheticism exalted a less crowded ideal. Favoring the pleasurable experience of art over its moral value, it emphasized private contemplation and singularity of experience. James gives voice to this ideal when he notes "There is no simpler pleasure than looking at a fine Titian." However, he adds "or than floating in a gondola . . . or taking one's coffee at Florian's." Aesthetic experience could be of anything; art had entered life to that degree. When, in his famous "Conclusion" to *The Renaissance*, Pater celebrated a consciousness that sought out experience as an end in itself and burned always like a "hard, gem-like flame," he was not that far from James' gondola-rider. But the inclusion within aesthetic experience of Venetian coffee-sipping repeats Ruskin's dilemma. Aesthetic pleasure might be available to anyone who could afford a gondola or a coffee on St Mark's Place, but, as a result, it ceased to be singular and original.

Meditation in a jostling crowd is difficult at best, as James himself notes on numerous occasions: "The sentimental tourist's only quarrel with Venice is that he has too many competitors there. He likes to be alone; to be original; to have (to himself, at least) the air of making discoveries . . . [T]he little wicket that admits you is perpetually turning and creaking, and you march through . . . with a herd of fellow-gazers. There is nothing left to discover or describe, and originality of attitude is completely impossible."

By entering circulation as a form of cultural capital, the ideal of aesthetic appreciation lost not only its uniqueness and originality but also its subversive power. As a celebration of sensuous experience, especially as it was most riotously embodied in the life of Wilde, it threatened Victorian respectability and morality. Just barely subliminal in its homoeroticism, its obvious delight in bodily pleasures was a scandal to the regime of Victorian sexual repression. But as a celebration of such potentially mass activities as gondola-riding, church-gazing, and coffee-sipping, it could be turned to uses more suited to the maintenance of the reigning stabilities. It diverted potentially troublesome energies into more pleasurable pastimes. Laboring classes on excursion were less likely to engage in "agitation."

How is aestheticism represented in "The Aspern Papers"? Look again at the passage in chapter 4 where the narrator thinks about the "moral fraternity" of devotees to art. Consider as well how the tale depicts the conflict between the singularity of aesthetic experience and a more public kind of appreciation. The contrast between Juliana and the narrator would again seem important. Note how her room is described and how her early life is characterized. Think again about how he and she represent contending attitudes towards the aesthetic.

8.4   Suggestions for an Historicist Reading of Elizabeth Bishop's "Twelve O'Clock News"

Bishop, after living in Brazil for nearly two decades, returned to the United States in the mid-1960s, in time to witness the public uprising against the Vietnam War. The Vietnamese had liberated their country by defeating the French in 1954 at Dien Bien Phu. The peace treaty that settled that struggle divided Vietnam between the North, controlled by the liberation forces, and the South, still essentially under colonial control. The government in the South was little more than a foreign-funded puppet regime, and the liberation forces continued to press the war, hoping to liberate the South as well. Throughout the 1950s and early 1960s, the US was drawn further into the war, first by sending advisors to aid the South Vietnamese Army, then by sending US Army troops to conduct the war themselves. Since the liberation forces were aided by Communist countries, the war became part of America's struggle against world Communism as that was embodied in the Soviet Union (made up of Russia and a number of other contiguous "republics"). But the war was widely perceived to be an illegitimate foreign intervention in a domestic civil war as well as an attempt to impose imperial will on a "backward" country.

Bishop's poem, she herself noted in an interview, is about the war, although she had written a first unsatisfactory draft while still in college in the 1930s. That draft never matured into a poem, and it seems to have required the combined experience of her time in Brazil, where she acquired firsthand knowledge of what it is to live in an underdeveloped country like Vietnam, and of the opposition to the Vietnam War on the part of friends like Mary McCarthy (with whom Bishop had lunch shortly before McCarthy left for one of her trips to Vietnam) to allow her to turn that early draft into a poem. A new historicist interest in the transverse connections between discourses might lead one to compare the poem to McCarthy's own writing on Vietnam. Here is an excerpt from her book on the war:

> The Saigonese themselves [Saigon was the capital of South Vietnam] are unaware of the magnitude of what is happening to their country, since they are unable to use military transport to get an aerial view of it; they only note the refugees sleeping in the streets and hear the B-52s pounding a few miles away. Seeing the war from the air, amid the crisscrossing Skyraiders, Supersabres, Phantoms, observation planes, Psywar planes (dropping leaflets), you ask yourself how much longer the Viet Cong can hold out; the country is so small that at the present rate of destruction there will be no place left for them to hide, not even under water, breathing through a straw. The plane and helicopter crews are alert for the slightest sign of movement in the fields and woods and estuaries below; they lean forward intently, scanning the ground. At night, the Dragon-ships come out, dropping flares and firing mini-guns.
>
> The Air Force seems inescapable, like the eye of God, and soon, you imagine (let us hope with hyperbole), all will be razed, charred, defoliated by that terrible searching gaze. Punishment can be magistral. A correspondent, who was tickled by the incident, described flying with a pilot of the little FAC plane that directs a big bombing mission; below, a lone Vietnamese on a bicycle stopped, looked up, dismounted, took up a rifle and fired; the pilot let him have it with the whole bombload of napalm – enough for a platoon. In such circumstances, anyone with a normal sense of fair play cannot help pulling for the bicyclist, but the sense of fair play, supposed to be Anglo-Saxon, has atrophied in the Americans here from lack of exercise. We draw a long face over Viet Cong "terror," but no one stops to remember that the Viet Cong does not possess that superior instrument of terror, an air force,

which in our case, over South Vietnam at least, is acting almost with impunity. The worst thing that could happen to our country would be to win this war.

Consider what connections can be made between this excerpt and Bishop's poem. Note how each one uses irony, and think about how Bishop might also be said, albeit implicitly, to rely on a notion of fair play.

The title "Twelve O'Clock News" refers to the fact that the reality of the war was mediated by television news. The poem therefore draws attention to the issue of representation – how do we know something foreign if we must know it through our own representations, our own concepts and mental images as well as our own media? The poem playfully describes objects on the writer's desk as if they were objects in the world. Consider how this strategy bears on the question of representation and knowledge. Think as well about how it is a comment on the war, on how and why it was conducted as it was.

A new historicist might claim that the poem, for all its subversiveness, is itself a move within power, a way for power to sanction itself. Can the poem be read in this way? Does it advance power while seeming to undermine it? Think of how the toleration of such criticism might lend legitimacy to military actions like the Vietnam War. The US military, after all, still supports and trains repressive military forces in places like the Middle East and Latin America. Does criticism simply make questionable actions seem more legitimate?

8.5   Suggestions for an Historicist Reading of *The Bluest Eye*

In the 1950s, blacks militated for change more forcefully than before, borrowing lessons from the successful campaign of nonviolent resistance by Indians against British colonial rule. By the 1960s, they had convinced the federal government to pass legislation outlawing racial discrimination. But poverty and economic racism remained obstacles for blacks, and there were a number of violent insurrections by blacks in the mid-1960s. These helped spur attempts at remediation on the part of the federal government, and as part of that effort, a study was conducted by the Department of Labor that would be called "The Moynihan Report," although its full title was "The Negro Family: A Case for National Action." The report, which appeared in March of 1965, describes in official social scientific language many things about black life that are described in fictional language by Morrison in her novel (1970). Indeed, passages from the report could easily serve as thematic glosses for the novel, although the report's controversial conclusion – that the matriarchal family structure that has resulted from the systematic dispossession of black men is one cause of the continuing culture of poverty amongst blacks – is probably not one Morrison would agree with.

Both the novel and the report might be said to share a rhetorical gesture of indictment and warning. Consider the following passage from the report: "At the heart of the deterioration of the fabric of Negro society is the deterioration of the Negro family. . . . There is probably no single fact of Negro American life so little understood by whites. . . . It is . . . difficult, however, for whites to perceive the effect that three centuries of exploitation have had on the fabric of Negro society itself. Here the consequences of the historic injustices done to Negro Americans are silent and hidden from view. But here is where the true injury has occurred: unless this damage is repaired, all the effort to end discrimination and poverty and injustice will come to little."

You might consider the relevance of this passage to the novel, especially the way the novel attempts to expose injuries that are "silent and hidden from view."

The report continues: "The Negro was given liberty, but not equality. Life remained hazardous and marginal. Of the greatest importance, the Negro male, particularly in the South, became an object of intense hostility, an attitude unquestionably based in some measure on fear. When Jim Crow [southern laws instituting segregation and denying equal rights to blacks] made its appearance towards the end of the 19th century, it may be speculated that it was the negro male who was most humiliated thereby; the male was more likely to use public facilities, which rapidly became segregated once the process began, and just as important, segregation and the submissiveness it exacts, are surely more destructive to the male than to the female personality. Keeping the Negro 'in his place' can be translated as keeping the Negro male in his place: the female was not a threat to anyone. Unquestionably, these events worked against the emergence of a strong father figure." The report suggests that slavery and economic distress after slavery worked to break down and interrupt the transmission of "appropriate nurturing behavior" from one generation of males to another in the black community: "Negro children without fathers flounder and fail."

Think about how this passage might be applied to the novel, and consider especially how Morrison depicts male characters like Cholly.

What do you think about the report's contention that "segregation and the submissiveness it exacts are surely more destructive to the male than to the female personality"? You might consider it in light of how Pauline and Pecola are depicted in the novel.

The report describes the negative effects of the displacement of rural black families from the South to urban settings in the North. It cites E. Franklin Frazier's study *The Negro Family*: "In many cases, of course, the dissolution of the simple family organization has begun before the family reaches the northern city. But, if these families have managed to preserve their integrity until they reach the northern city, poverty, ignorance, and color force them to seek homes in deteriorated slum areas from which practically all institutional life has disappeared. Hence, at the same time that these simple rural families are losing their internal cohesion, they are being freed from the controlling force of public opinion and communal institutions. Family desertion among negroes in cities appears, then, to be one of the inevitable consequences of the impact of urban life on the simple family organization and folk culture which the negro has evolved in the rural South." Consider the trajectory of the Breedlove family in terms of this passage. Think as well about how folk culture is depicted. What role does it seem to play in southern black life?

The report argues that the disastrously high unemployment levels for black males has a negative effect on the family's integrity. Men, who are socialized to "strut," are denied dignity and a sense of worth, and when women become the breadwinners for the family, this further erodes their sense of self. The report cites Thomas Pettigrew: "The Negro wife in this situation can easily become disgusted with her financially dependent husband, and her rejection of him further alienates the male from family life." Think about the relations between Pauline and Cholly in this context. Does the novel bear out or further complicate this contention?

You might also consider the following citation in the report from Richard Cloward and Robert Ontell: "We are plagued in work with these [black] youth, by what appears to be a low tolerance for frustration. They are not able to absorb setbacks. Minor irritants and rebuffs are magnified out of all proportion to reality. Perhaps they react as they do because they are not equal to the world that confronts them, and they know it. And it is the knowing that is devastating." How might we say of Cholly that the "knowing . . . is devastating"?

Finally, how might the novel be read as refuting the findings of the report?

CHAPTER 9

Ethnic, Post-Colonial, and International Studies

9.1 Introduction

The last half of the twentieth century witnessed the end of the colonial domination of large parts of the world by European countries like France and England. Most previously colonized countries achieved independence. During the same period, ethnic groups who lived in situations of diasporic dispersal – Africans in the United States, for example – struggled to end longstanding practices of racist mistreatment and to achieve equality with local ethnic majorities. In this evolving geopolitical situation, attention turned to the differences in literature and culture between the various ethnic groups around the world, as well as to the way literature engages such issues as inter-ethnic relations, racial identity, homeland, exile, diaspora, nationhood, and the like. In situations of severe racial oppression like the United States and South Africa, literature came to be seen as a privileged site for understanding the social structures, cultural codes, and psychological tropes of cross-cultural and inter-ethnic understanding and misunderstanding.

While science casts doubt on the idea that the human species divides into ethnicities and races, race and ethnicity remain powerful cultural and social categories. And while external traits such as skin color cannot be construed as expressing internal ethnic essences or separable genetic identities, they are nevertheless the visual language of human difference and human community. They are why people band together or fall apart, even if the racial identities they supposedly represent have no existence apart from the differences in legible traits. Moreover, history speaks a different language from science, and to read a work of literature in English by someone of "color" is to read something marked generally by a history of mistreatment, disenfranchisement, and dispossession. Race and ethnicity, in other words, for all their imaginary qualities, are not erasable marks. Rather, they are one of the most effective and compelling determinants of cultural difference and of literary specificity. To read Toni Morrison's *Beloved*, to take one of the most celebrated examples of the late twentieth century, is necessarily to ask what it means to be black and African descended in a largely white America and what responsibilities are borne by those who are white, regardless of whether or not those accidental external colors express any innate or essential genetic difference. It is to ask how the long history of mistreatment of one social group by another weighs upon the present. And it is to confront the ghosts of one's culture, the ghost of the overseer and the ghost of the slave, as well as to remember what shouldn't be forgotten.

Literary criticism that takes race and ethnicity as its principle concern has helped foreground the importance of racial identification in society and question the hitherto unquestioned ethnic norms of racially unmarked literary study. The emergence of ethnic criticism displaced the notion that universality spoke a white dialect, and it focused attention on the bleaching out of other-than-dominant ethnic experiences by the privilege, always implicit and sometimes explicit, given whiteness in Eurocentric and North American literary study. Two major consequences of this change are the recognition of the importance of ignored ethnic experiences and literatures and the reconsideration of the history of white discourse from an interracial perspective. The new ethnic criticism explores ethnic identities whose cultures had been marginalized if not entirely ignored during the era of white normativity. And by exploring the history of the various ethnicities and of their lives together, it destabilizes the moral self-assurance of white European-descended culture. Like Feminism, Ethnic Studies obliges the canon (mainly male, mainly white) to take stock of its imbrication with the violent subordination of others. As undergraduates, we all read Conrad's *Heart of Darkness* for its ambiguity, not for its call for a more authentic, manly, and violent imperialism. Times have changed, and with change come new questions: how might a work like *Heart of Darkness* have helped foster and maintain negative and harmful racialist attitudes and stereotypes? How might the entire canon be reconsidered with the same question in mind? How might the introduction of literature to the canon by or about people of color mitigate the harmful effects of such cultural imperialism?

9.2   A Post-Colonial Reading of Elizabeth Bishop's "Brazil, January 1, 1502"

Bishop's poem is about the Portuguese conquest of Brazil, a conquest whose rapaciously sexual character resulted eventually in the near elimination of the indigenous population. The poem is also about how European culture fosters such imperialism. In a gesture found elsewhere in Bishop's work, she literalizes a metaphor, that which would compare a natural landscape to a tapestry. She chooses as her epigraph phrases from Kenneth Clark's art criticism – "embroidered nature . . . tapestried landscape" – and she assumes the stance of someone studying a tapestry depicting Brazil at the time of the European conquest from the standpoint of its Portuguese colonizers. The poem thus takes its departure from a familiar Bishop concern with the mesh of representation and reality (or of the mistaking of representation for reality) and inflects that concern toward a criticism of the Europeans who brought to the New World cultural images that legitimated the violent subordination of the indigenous peoples. The assimilation of the other world and the other people to one's own categories of understanding (in this instance, aesthetic and moral categories) is compared to the attempt to assimilate other people to one's own ethnic group through sexual conquest.

The title makes clear that Bishop's topic is an historical event, the conquest of Brazil by Portugal, yet her epigraph underscores her interest in how representation mediates both our knowledge of such realities and those realities themselves. We know history only as representation (hence the stance of viewing a tapestry instead of the "actual events"), but the Portuguese themselves perceived the indigenous peoples through lenses that were themselves tinted by representations learned in their own culture that they carried with them to the New World. Representation inheres in our experience of things, and fabrications ("embroidered," "tapestried") are part of knowing the world. If we always know through previously formulated conceptions, then knowing is difficult to separate from art. Not only is the landscape like a tapestry, but also our knowledge of it is a kind of tapestry, a picture at a distance that stands between the thing and us. Looking at things is looking at pictures of things. This problem or difficulty of knowledge moves a writer like Bishop to devote as much attention and care as she does to the exact description of objects, a task that, in light of the imperialist venture she describes in this poem, takes on a political relevance it might otherwise have seemed to lack. But it also enables conquerors to take pictures for things and to mistake their own conceptions for reality. The result is violence done to others in an imperialist conquest carried out in the name of a Christian conception of the world.

Bishop begins by juxtaposing the present and the past – "Januaries" – so that her own experience is immediately compared to the experience of the European conquerors. But the sameness of experience is not simple, and Bishop immediately complicates what she seems to assert: "Nature greets our eyes / exactly as she must have greeted theirs." One might initially think that Bishop is pointing out how nature has not changed since the European conquest in 1502, but she capitalizes "Nature" as if it is not nature as such but Nature as an allegorical emblem that she has in mind. At the time of the conquest, European art forms like the tapestry were characterized by allegory, a mode of representation that substituted emblems or representational figures for ideas or things. "Nature" might be represented by emblems like trees or flowers, while a noble and strong-looking character in armor might stand for "Virtue." In parallel fashion, nature was thought to be itself symbolic. Divinity especially manifested itself in nature, and natural objects could be interpreted as signs of moral qualities or of divine intent. By capitalizing Nature, Bishop suggests that what the Europeans encountered in Brazil was an already allegorized nature, one transformed into their own way of picturing the world as a place full of meanings.

That Bishop describes the world as if it were a tapestry that represents Brazil at the time of the conquest adds another meaning to the dual temporality of "Januaries" and "exactly as." The past time is captured and held in the image of the tapestry; we in the present can see exactly what they saw in the past by looking at the image, since it shows how they saw nature. But meaning flows in an opposed direction as well: what they saw is not pictured; rather it was a picture. By looking at a picture, we see what they saw. The third line is telling in this regard: "every square inch filling in with foliage." There is nothing that is not representation; nature itself cannot be seen or grasped; rather, "Nature" represented by "big leaves, little leaves, and giant leaves," whose exaggeration and multiplicity suggest representational excess, obliterate what of nature might have been seen. Bishop's description of colors – "blue, blue-green, and olive" – further distances the natural and underscores how representational surfaces with their illogical and nonrealistic color choices occupy attention. The choice of "satin" in line seven further emphasizes just how cultural this nature is, how much an expression of civilized codes and ideals. A sense of the unnaturalness of "Nature" is further emphasized in the remainder of the stanza until Bishop concludes by making the theme of the artfulness of imperial perception explicit: she compares the nature depicted to a tapestry just "taken off the frame."

Bishop in the second stanza more expressly engages the allegorical character of representation. The broken wheel, an emblem of the absence or failure of civilization, suggests that Nature is a realm resistant to imperial domestication, a realm whose power is indicated by "the big symbolic birds." It now becomes clear that overgrown nature is for the Christian conquerors an emblem of sexual temptation and moral transgression. Bishop notes "five sooty dragons near some massy rocks" who are meant to represent "Sin." But why they are Sin is not at once clear; Bishop leaves the attribution of meaning unjustified, thus underscoring its allegorical character. Allegories do not require the provision of definitions because they are representational forms whose codes or dictionaries are already understood by their audience. Any cultured Portuguese looking at this "picture" of the landscape would understand the dragon as an emblem of "Sin."

Bishop describes nature as at once out of control and "neat." It is at war within itself – "overlapping," "attacked above," and "scaling-ladder vines." The war is between natural growths like lichens that create "gray moonbursts" like explosions and the vines that are "oblique and neat" and that allow an easy tally of moral yes's and no's in the language of the conquerors – "'one leaf yes and one leaf no' (in Portuguese)." The "hell-green flames" of the moss suggest the Christian concept of divine punishment for sin, but Bishop's use of the adjective "lovely" to describe them intimates her own quite different sense of what such natural events might mean. By juxtaposing hell, a term that usually evokes the color red, and green, the color of natural growth, Bishop makes the moral categories of Christian theology that appear in the assignment of the moral meaning "Sin" to a natural object seem a perverse addition to nature, an attempt at discoloration as distortive as the odd blues and satins of the previous stanza. But red is there as well in the stanza's concluding description of the dragons' sexual desire for the female lizard. For Christianity, sex is Sin, yet Bishop renders difficult such moral categorization by using the word "wicked" – a word both of moral condemnation and of hip post-moralistic approval – to characterize the female's sexuality – "her wicked tail straight up and over." And the line "red as a red-hot wire" suggests something that glows positively rather than something worthy of negative moral judgment.

One purpose of Christian theology was to allow believers to stand above nature, to separate themselves from the temptations of sexual desires located in bodily nature. By describing such moral categories as if they were in a tapestry, Bishop is also suggesting that those categories were artful representations of the world which coded it in certain ways (Sin for sex, Virtue for conquest). Her description of nature, however, suggests that it consists of powerful forces, sexuality among them, that threaten to overwhelm such categorical guardrails. If indeed sexuality is nature, and if nature is of a wildness not easily denied or controlled, then the moral categorizers will themselves be vulnerable to its power.

This is what Bishop argues in the final stanza. Having described the dragons' sexual desire for the female lizard, she says "Just so the Christians." And she adds what is probably her own assessment of them – "hard as nails" – a characterization whose significance is underscored by Bishop's ascription of a delicacy to nature at odds with the Christians' hardness – "a simple web," "feathery detail," "swarthy, squat, but delicate," etc. Nature is complex and varied while Christian theology imposes on it hard moral distinctions such as "Sin." The comparative proportions of the figures in the imaginary tapestry allow Bishop to mix assessment and description when she characterizes the Christians as being "tiny as nails." In nature and compared to nature, they are small, but they "found it all," a formulation which suggests how totalizing the allegorical moral picture that the Christians painted of the world is. There are no empty spaces, no unaccounted-for parts, no ungrasped and unassimilated natural objects. All can be absorbed and adjusted to the positive/negative, yes/no grid of Christian moral categories. This is why the world found in Brazil is "not unfamiliar." It fits into an already formulated allegorical code for understanding the world that the Europeans brought with them on their ships and in their minds.

Yet, Bishop carefully notes, the world met did not in fact correspond to the European picture of Nature: "no lovers' walks, no bowers / no cherries to be picked, no lute music." For the Europeans of 1502, nature – as known through tapestries and paintings – was pastoral, a place of bowers and shepherds' lutes. Bishop suggests that they could not understand the New World precisely because of such pre-installed categories, such portable pictures of the world. The world does not correspond to their allegorical mode of moral representation, yet for that very reason, it must be forced to correspond. By inserting "cherries to be picked," a coarse colloquial term for the first rupture of the hymen in sexual copulation, Bishop undermines the pastoral imagery and romantic idealism of European allegorical art by noting the natural physicality it masks, a physicality to which she soon again alludes when she points out that the Europeans nevertheless found in Brazil something that corresponded to their dreams "of wealth and luxury . . . plus a brand-new pleasure." That pleasure is the rape of Indian women. The hypocrisy of raping indigenous women while pretending to bring them Christian salvation is captured in the line "Directly after Mass." The Christian soldiers are described as ripping "into the hanging fabric," as tearing apart the moral picture or tapestry of the world they brought with them, thus betraying their own moral ideals. But the phrase also suggests the way that their grasp of the world, their translation of it into their own codes, was itself a violation of that world, a destruction of what made it beautiful or comparable to a tapestry.

The significance of Bishop's deliberate confusion of the representational and the real, the picture and the world pictured, now becomes more clear. If the "hanging fabric" is the picture of the world the Europeans brought with them, it is also the natural world as art, as something characterized by delicate work and beauty. This is assimilated to the imaginary European tapestry that is the occasion of the poem, but it is there as background to the moral allegory the Christians find in Nature, the coding of Sin as female sexuality, for example. The irreducible otherness of nature, its outsideness in relation to all cultural representations and all categories of understanding, especially the allegorical ones of the conquering Europeans, leaves its trace or mark on those representations. Unassimilable, it appears nevertheless as the desired yet unattainable object, the female lizard who evokes desire yet remains out of reach.

The careful staging of these varied, crossed meanings allows Bishop in the end to maintain an opening against imperial violence. The Indian women call to each other, breaking the silence of the tapestry and posing a counterpoint to the Christian moral allegory which Bishop now imagines being transformed – "or had the birds waked up?" If Christian allegorizing imposes silence so that its highly codified visual meanings, which are comparable to a species of writing in that significance is determined by reference to something else, can be kept dominant, then verbal expression takes on the radical significance of waking up slumbering colonized communities that had been silenced into submission to the Christian worldview.

The women also, of course, form a community of resistance, a subjectivity resistant to the objectification of the tapestry of colonial understanding and representation. That subjectivity emerges as the possibility that the background for the allegory, the birds, for example, who had passively served as vehicles for the meanings of the Christian worldview, might suddenly burst into life, cease being silent vehicles. That the women are described as "retreating, always retreating" suggests that the appropriate strategy of resistance in the face of a more powerful allegorizing vision is to subtract oneself from the allegory, to step out of the imperialists' moral picture of the world, and to go "behind it." Because the allegory is a total one, resistance has to be outside the picture; it has to consist of a refusal of the very act of understanding and representation the Europeans bring with them. The indigenous people will always for the Europeans be unrepresentable, unassimilable to a moral allegorical mode of representation or picturing that fits new experiences, objects, and events into already codified modes of understanding. In themselves, as resistant subjects, they can only exist outside or "behind."

Bishop depicts the imperial imagination as one that is trapped in its own presuppositions and expectations and that is incapable of understanding the world in other terms. It is also a moral imagination whose assumptions seem to make hypocrisy inevitable. As physical beings, the Christian imperialists inhabit the nature of sexual desire, yet by allegorically representing such desire as Sin and pretending to inhabit a moral picture of the world that assumes their own virtue and others' depravity, they leave themselves open to the significant moral failing that sexual imperialism carried out in the name of the superiority of Christian European civilization was. For Bishop, the European conquest of Brazil is a continuation into explicit sexual violation of implicit sexual violence of the European Renaissance male literary and artistic tradition of romantic love, whose central narrative is the male conquest of women ("cherries to be picked"). Bishop's references to "lovers' walks" and "bowers" might seem distant from the issue of military imperialism. But by connecting that romantic cultural tradition to an "old dream of wealth and luxury," she creates a link between the literary/artistic form and male control over social wealth and power. The conquest of women in romantic narrative guise is part of the luxury made possible to men by wealth. It is for these reasons that Bishop carefully juxtaposes "wealth, plus a brand-new pleasure." The poem suggests that economic power cohabits with sexual power, and the way the imperial quest for wealth was conjoined with the sexual exploitation of native women merely continues a connection already established in European society at the time, a connection made explicit in art works like tapestries that were tokens of wealth and luxury and that frequently depicted romantic themes. Such romantic picturing masked the sexual physicality that underlay the depictions, and such masking, a poem like "Brazil" seems to suggest, merely allowed Europeans to lie to themselves about their most intimate motives.

9.3   Suggestions for an Ethnic Studies Reading of Elizabeth Bishop's "Faustina, or Rock Roses"

Bishop wrote a number of poems that deal with ethnicity. Two of them – "Cootchie" and "Faustina" – concern black women servants. "Songs for a Colored Singer," a poem Bishop imagined as a blues song for Billie Holliday, can be read in juxtaposition to "Strange Fruit," a Holliday song about lynching. While living in Brazil, Bishop wrote several poems about poor blacks, including "The Burglar of Babylon," an indictment of the Brazilian military, and "Squatter's Children."

You might focus on "Faustina," a poem that concerns a visit by the speaker of the poem to a sick white woman who is tended by a black servant named Faustina. Begin with the way the white woman's room is described and notice how Bishop inflects description toward psychological and social meanings – for example, the bulb which "betrays us all." Notice as well the role colors play, white especially. Given the emphasis on whiteness, it's interesting that when Faustina appears she's described as having a "sinister kind face" which "presents a cruel black / coincident conundrum." What do you think Bishop means by this? She goes on to say that the conundrum poses a choice of interpretation between a "dream of protection and rest" and a nightmare "that never before dared last / more than a second." What nightmare might Bishop be alluding to?

You might also think about how this question bears on the relationship between whites and blacks in general. It might be interesting to compare the poem to Eric Sundquist's essay on Melville's *Benito Cereno* (in *Literary Theory: An Anthology*).

9.4 Suggestions for an Ethnic Studies Reading of *The Bluest Eye*

The ideology of race allows people to differentiate themselves from others, even within the same supposed ethnic group. You might consider how the novel deals with such issues. Think of the characters of Geraldine and Maureen Peel and how they differentiate themselves from Claudia, Frieda, and Pecola. Does Morrison explain why they do this?

Ethnic marking can obviously be harmful. Pecola suffers most from the markings of ethnicity, while Claudia seems determined to transform their meaning and Pauline adjusts herself to them. Consider how Morrison differentiates the three characters and their differing relationships to their ethnic identities.

Consider the following from the final section of the novel: "A little black girl yearns for the blue eyes of a little white girl, and the horror at the heart of her yearning is exceeded only by the evil of fulfillment." Morrison seems to be suggesting that blacks should not allow the dominant white culture to script their identities. At the end of the 1960s, when the novel was written, many blacks were countering the dominant white culture's negative image of blacks by affirming more positive and enabling images in the black pride movement. How might the story of Pecola's desire for the bluest eye be understood in light of this historical development?

Index

The Adventures of Huckleberry Finn (Twain), 4
aesthetic movement, 139, 141–2
American New Critics, 1, 90; and Marxism, 6; and paradox, 5; New Critical reading of "At the Fishhouses," 24; New Critical reading of *King Lear*, 11–12; New Critical reading of "The Moose," 23; and universal meanings, 4–5, 12; and verbal patterns/texture, 5; *see also* Formalism; Russian Formalists
Annales school, 129
"The Aspern Papers" (James), 53; aestheticism in, 139, 141–2; bodily decay in, 106–7, 110; boundaries in, 108–9, 112–13; capitalism in, 62–3; dangerous duality in, 105–6; diffusion of identity in, 108–9; feminist reading of, 104–13; historicist reading of, 139, 141–2; ideal v. fallen world in, 111–12; male identity in, 109–10, 112–13; Marxist reading of, 62–3; negative image of women, 104–5; negative/positive aspects in, 110; psychoanalytic reading of, 50–1; psychosexual imagery in, 107; Structuralist reading of, 33; tourist theme in, 139, 141–2
"At the Fishhouses" (Bishop):

alternation/repetition in, 24–5; formalist reading of, 24–5; religious metaphors in, 24

Bakhtin, Mikhail, 3–4, 10–11
Basilikon Doron (James I), 131, 133–4
Bataille, Georges, 70–1
Baudrillard, Jean, 72, 74, 75, 89
Beloved (Morrison), 148
Benito Cereno (Melville), 155
Benjamin, Walter, 64
Bishop, Elizabeth, 53; concern with Vietnam, 142–4; ethnic reading of, 154–5; feminist reading of, 113–14; formalist reading of, 12–23; gender reading of, 126–7; historicist reading of, 143, 144; Marxist reading of, 64; post-colonial reading of, 149–54; Post-Structuralist reading of, 89–98; psychoanalytic reading of, 38–43; Structuralist reading of, 34
The Bluest Eye (Morrison): desire and denial in, 45, 47–9; disempowerment in, 100; ethnic reading of, 155; feminist reading of, 114; gender reading of, 127; historicist reading of, 144–6; Marxist reading of, 65–6; Moynihan Report as inspiration for, 144–6; opposites in, 98–9; personal/

social conflict in, 44–7; positive/
negative images in, 155; Post-
Structuralist reading of, 98–100;
psychoanalytic reading of, 44–9; race/
class oppression in, 65–6; as realist
novel, 99; sexual identity and practice
in, 127; territorialization in, 99–100
Bordo, Susan, 114
Bowen, Catherine Drinker, 131
Bray, Alan, 118
"Brazil, January 1, 1502": Christianity
in, 151–2, 153; crossed meanings in,
153; historical representation in, 149;
imperial imagination in, 154;
juxtaposition of present and past in,
150; Nature in, 150–1, 152; post-
colonial reading of, 149–54; sexuality
in, 151–3, 154; women as community
of resistance in, 153–4; world as a
tapestry in, 149, 150
Brooks, Cleanth, 5, 24, 89
"The Burglar of Babylon" (Bishop),
155
Byron, George, Lord, 139

Cervantes, Miguel de, 3
Chaucer, Geoffrey, 124
Cixous, Hélène, 74–5
Clark, Kenneth, 149
Coleridge, Samuel Taylor, 89
Conrad, Joseph, 2, 148
Cook, Thomas, 140
"Cootchie" (Bishop), 154
"Crusoe in England" (Bishop): allusion
to Wordsworth in, 94; deconstructive
perspective on, 90–1, 96–7; informal
narrative mode in, 92–3; Post-
Structuralist reading of, 89–97;
representation in, 91–2; Romanticism
in, 91–7; and Shelley, 95; truth and
meaning in, 90–1

deconstruction, 71–4, 90–1, 96–7, 129; in
The Bluest Eye, 99; in "Crusoe in
England," 90–1, 96–7; in *King Lear*,
79–88

Deleuze, Gilles, 74, 76, 99
Demonologie (James I), 131, 133, 134
Derrida, Jacques, viii, 71, 72–4, 76,
79–80, 96
Don Quixote (Cervantes), 3

Eliot, T.S., 2
Ethnic Studies: applied to *The Bluest
Eye*, 155; applied to "Faustina, or
Rock Roses," 154–5; emergence of,
147–8

"Faustina, or Rock Roses" (Bishop):
ethnic reading of, 154–5; role of color
in 155
feminism, 74–5; Anglo-American, 103–4;
applied to "The Aspern Papers,"
104–13; applied to *The Bluest Eye*,
114; applied to *King Lear*, 113;
applied to "Roosters," 113–14;
French, 102–3; historical, 104;
patriarchal aspect of, 101–2, 103–4;
and subordination of women, 101, 103
Formalism: American, 4–5; applied to
"At the Fishhouses," 24–5; applied to
King Lear, 6–12; applied to "The
Moose," 12–23; criticism of, 6;
defined, 1–2; as first step in study of
literature, 2; Russian, 2–4; *see also*
American New Critics; Russian
Formalists
Foucault, Michel, 71, 77, 115, 129
Freudianism, 35–6, 37; applied to "The
Aspern Papers," 50–1; *see also*
psychoanalysis

Gallagher, Catherine, 128
Gay/Lesbian Theory, 115–17; *see also*
Gender Studies; Queer Theory
Geertz, Clifford, 129
Gender Studies, 115; and alternative
sexual practices, 116–17; and
heterosexual/homosexual opposition,
116; and notion of sexual identity,
115–16; and structure of male
heterosexual oppression, 117; *see also*

Gay/Lesbian Theory; Queer Theory
Greenblatt, Stephen, 128, 129–30
Guattari, Felix, 74, 76, 99

Hamlet (Shakespeare), 1
Harriot, Thomas, 129
Hawthorne, Nathaniel, 2, 5
Heart of Darkness (Conrad), 148; formal
    arrangement of, 2
Henry plays (Shakespeare), 129–30
Hernstein, Richard, 66
historicism: applied to "The Aspern
    Papers," 139–42; applied to *The Bluest
    Eye*, 144–6; applied to *King Lear*,
    131–39; applied to "Twelve O'Clock
    News," 143, 144; and historical
    research, 131; new, 128–31; and
    power, 129–30, 131; relationship with
    literature, 130–1; and representation,
    129–30, 131; rise and fall of, 128

ideology, 53, 54; applied to *King Lear*,
    60–2
"In the Village" (Bishop): displacement
    in, 38–40; psychoanalytic reading of,
    38–40
"In the Waiting Room" (Bishop): gender
    reading of, 126–7; issue of identity in,
    126–7
Irigaray, Luce, 72, 74–5, 113

Jakobson, Roman, 2, 26, 71
James, Henry, 53; feminist reading of,
    104–13; historicist reading of, 139–42;
    Marxist reading of, 62–3; modernism
    of, 63; psychoanalytic reading of,
    50–1; Structuralist reading of, 33
James I, King: attitude to law and
    monarchical power, 135–8; as bad-
    mannered, 132; conflict with Edward
    Coke, 131, 135; dislike of court style,
    132–3; dislike of women, 134; as
    father and king, 137; literary works,
    131, 133–4; person and court of
    paralleled in *King Lear*, 2, 131–9
Jessie, J.H., 131

Keats, John, 89
King Lear (Shakespeare), 53, 69, 131; at
    juncture of feudalism and capitalism,
    55, 56–60; authoritative discourse in,
    10; bawdy language in, 8; compulsory
    heterosexuality in, 119–20, 122–3,
    125, 126; concerned with rebellion
    and hospitality, 132, 137; counterfeit
    in, 89; deconstructive perspective in,
    79–88; defamiliarization in, 6–7;
    dialogization in, 10–11; double plot
    in, 29–31; feminist reading of, 113;
    feminization of men in, 120–2, 124;
    formal arrangement of, 1; gender
    reading of, 118–26; hidden intentions
    in, 9; historicist reading of, 131–9;
    homosexuality in, 118–19, 122–6;
    homosocial relationships in, 122–3;
    how studied, 2; ideological aspects of,
    60–2; indirect presentation in, 7–8;
    linguistic duality in, 8–9; Marxist
    reading of, 54–62; meaning system
    of, 30–2; monarchical power/judicial
    authority in, 137–9; New Critical
    reading of, 11–12; and parallels with
    court of King James, 131–9; parental
    authority/filial loyalty in, 134;
    patriarchy in, 113; plainness and
    abstinence in, 133–4; Post-
    Structuralist reading of, 76–89;
    power in, 100; psychoanalytic reading
    of, 49–50; punishment/discipline in,
    77–8; Russian Formalist reading of,
    6–11; Structuralist reading of, 28,
    29–32; territorialization in, 76–8;
    truth and signification in, 76, 78,
    80–8
Knox, John, 113
Kristeva, Julia, 71, 74, 76, 78, 99
Kuhl, E.P., 128

Lacan, Jacques, 37–8
language: deconstruction of, 72–4; as
    representation, 72; signs/signifiers in,
    27–9; as subject to contingency,
    indeterminacy, and generation of

multiple meanings, 67; as synchronic/
diachronic, 27; and the unconscious,
38
lesbian studies *see* Gay/Lesbian Theory
Lévi-Strauss, Claude, 34
Literary Research Guide (Patterson), 131
literature: form expresses content/
content as effect of form, 1; formalist
approach to, 1–2, 6; location within
social, economic, historical context,
53–4; manifest/latent levels of, 26–7,
28; New Critical approach to, 4–5;
psychoanalytic issues, 38; and reality,
69; relationship with history, 130–1;
Russian Formalist approach to, 2–4;
study of, 2; *see also* novels
logocentrism, 90
Lyotard, Jean-François, 72, 74, 75,
76, 88

McCarthy, Mary, 143–4
"The Map" (Bishop), Structuralist
reading of, 34
Marcuse, Herbert, 64
Marx, Karl, 52–3
Marxism, 52–3, 128, 130; applied to
"The Aspern Papers," 62–3; applied
to *The Bluest Eye*, 65–6; applied to
King Lear, 54–62; applied to "A
Miracle for Breakfast," 64; theory of
history, 54–6; two forms of, 53–4
Mauss, Marcel, 70
Melville, Herman, 155
Miller, D.A., 128
"A Miracle for Breakfast" (Bishop), 53;
Marxist reading of, 64; social criticism
in, 64
Montrose, Louis, 128
"The Moose" (Bishop): alternation of
sounds in, 14–15; ambivalence in, 17;
delayed presentation of subject in, 13;
displacement in, 40; form of, 13;
formalist reading of, 12–23; Marxist
reading of, 64; mirroring in, 14;
negative images in, 16; New Critical
reading of, 23; observation/

description in, 12; passivity of subject
in, 15; as poem on death, 12–13, 15,
16, 20–1; psychoanalytic reading of,
40; religious symbolism in, 17;
repetition in, 18–20; rhyme, rhythm,
alliteration in, 14, 18, 22–3; Russian
Formalist reading of, 23; time/
eternity in, 21–2; transformation of
images in, 15–17
Morrison, Toni, 148; ethnic reading of,
155; feminist reading of, 114; gender
reading of, 127; historicist reading of,
144–6; Marxist reading of, 65–6; Post-
Structuralist reading of, 98–100;
psychoanalytic reading of, 44–9
Moynihan Report (1965), 144–6
Murray, Charles, 66

Negro Americans, report on, 144–6
New Critics, *see* American New Critics
new historicists, *see* historicism
Nietzsche, Friedrich, 69–70, 90
novels: carnivalesque, 4; as heteroglossic,
4; picaresque, 3; quest romance, 3;
realist, 99; *see also* literature

object relations theory, 36–7; applied to
"The Aspern Papers," 51
"Ode on a Grecian Urn" (Keats), 89
"Ode to the West Wind" (Shelley), 95
"Over, 2000 Illustrations and a
Complete Concordance" (Bishop),
Post-Structuralist reading of, 98

Pater, Walter, 141
patriarchy, 101–2, 103–4; in *King Lear*,
113; in "Roosters," 113–14
Plato, 82
poetry: incarnational theory of, 89–90;
Marxist view of, 64; as monological,
4; paradox in, 5; rhythm and sound
in, 3, 4
Popish Impostures (Harsnett), 131
Portraits of Place (James), 141
Post-Colonialism, applied to "Brazil,
January 1, 1502" (Bishop), 149–54

Post-Modernism, 75–6

Post-Structuralism, 129; applied to *The Bluest Eye*, 98–100; applied to "Crusoe in England," 89–97; applied to *King Lear*, 76–89; applied to "Over, 2000 Illustrations and a Complete Concordance," 98; concerned with identity, undecidability of meaning, and indeterminacy, 67–9; and deconstruction, 71–4; and differentiation, 72–4; and feminism, 74–5; influence of Bataille on, 70–1; and knowledge in society, 71; and madness, 70–1; Nietzschean, 69–70; and Post-Modernism, 75–6; and reality, 69; and signification, 71–3; truth and ideation, 68–70; truth and meaning, 72–4

Prague Linguists, 71

Propp, Vladimir, 26–7, 33

psychoanalysis: applied to "The Aspern Papers," 50–1; applied to *The Bluest Eye*, 44–9; applied to "In the Village," 38–40; applied to *King Lear*, 49–50; applied to "The Moose," 40; applied to reading strategies, 38; applied to "Sestina," 40–3; defined, 35; Freudian, 35–6, 37; Lacanian, 37–8; object relations theory, 36–7; *see also* Freudianism

Ptolemy, 128

Queer Theory, 117–18; *see also* Gay/Lesbian Theory; Gender Studies

race, *see* Ethnic Studies

rationalism, 129

Renaissance discourse, 118–19, 121, 122–3, 130

The Renaissance (Pater), 141

Romantics, 89–97

"Roosters" (Bishop): feminist reading of, 113–14; male/female perspective in, 113–14

Ruskin, John, 141

Russian Formalists, 71; form makes possible new content, 3; form subsumes content, 3; and novelistic discourse, 5; origins, 2–3; and poetic discourse, 3, 12; reading of "At the Fishhouses," 24; reading of *King Lear*, 6–11; reading of "The Moose," 23; *see also* American New Critics; Formalism

Saussure, Ferdinand de, 27–8, 34

The Scarlet Letter (Hawthorne), 5; formal arrangement of, 2

semiotics, 75–6, 78

"Sestina" (Bishop): displacement in, 41–3; psychoanalytic reading of, 40–3; separation and loss in, 40–3

Shakespeare, William, 1, 2, 53, 128, 129–30, 131; as critical of judges and justices, 135–9; feminist reading of, 113; gender reading of, 118–26; historicist reading of, 131–9; Marxist reading of, 54–62; New Critical reading of, 11–12; Post-Structuralist reading of, 76–89; and presentation of King James as Lear, 131–9; psychoanalytic reading of, 49–50; Russian Formalist reading of, 6–11; Structuralist reading of, 28, 29–32

"The Shampoo" (Bishop), 126

Shelley, Percy Bysshe, 95

Shklovsky, Viktor, 2

Slack, Paul, 131

"Songs for a Colored Singer" (Bishop), 154

"Squatter's Children" (Bishop), 155

Stephen, Leslie, 140

Stone, Lawrence, 131

The Stones of Venice (Ruskin), 141

Structuralism: applied to "The Aspern Papers," 33; applied to *King Lear*, 29–32; applied to "The Map," 34; concern with properties of literature, 26–7; defined, 67; origin of, 27; Saussurean, 27–8

Sundquist, Eric, 155

Tomashevsky, Boris, 2
tourist industry, 62, 139–41
Transatlantic Sketches (James), 140
The True Lawe of Free Monarchies
  (James I), 131, 135–6
Twain, Mark, 4
"Twelve O'Clock News" (Bishop),

historicist reading of, 143, 144

Vietnam, 142–4

The Waste Land (Eliot), 2
Wordsworth, William, 24, 89–90, 94
Wuthering Heights (Brontë), 1–2

LITERARY THEORY

LITERARY THEORY
An Anthology

Edited by Julie Rivkin and Michael Ryan
Connecticut College; Northeastern University, Boston

Literary Theory: An Anthology is a unique combination of the classic statements in criticism and the new theories that have revolutionized literary study in the past several decades. This unprecedented collection will be an invaluable reference tool for students interested in acquiring a comprehensive knowledge of the most recent developments in critical theory while becoming expert in the tradition from which the new theories derive.

The anthology contains classic texts from Formalism, Structuralism, Marxism, Psychoanalysis, Deconstruction, Historicism, and Feminism, and it includes cutting-edge work by leading theoreticians in such fields as Post-Modernism, Cultural Studies, Post-Colonial Criticism, Gay/Lesbian Studies, Ethnic Studies, and Film. The anthology constitutes the most comprehensive collection of schools and methods that make up the rich and exciting field of literary and cultural studies.

229 x 152mm / 6 x 9in   1168 pages

0-631-20028-2 hardback
0-631-20029-0 paperback

December 1997

TO ORDER CALL :
1-800-216-2522 (N. America orders only) or
24-hour freephone on 0500 008205
(UK orders only)

VISIT US ON THE WEB : http://www.blackwellpublishers.co.uk